CONTENTS

ALABAMA JUBILEE

Words by JACK YELLEN
Music by GEORGE COBB

G7
C
gin - ia who is past eight - y three,
Shout - in' "I'm full o' pep!
Guitar Tacet
(Spoken)
A7
Watch yo' step, watch yo' step!" One leg - ged Joe danced a - roun' on his toe,
Dm
A7
Dm
D7
D7-5
Threw a - way his crutch and hol - lered, "Let 'er go!" Oh, hon - ey,
C
E7
F
C
D7
Hail! Hail! the gang's all here for an Al - a - ba - ma
G7
1 C
Cdim
G7
2 C
G7
C
Jub - i - lee You ought to lee.

ALL MY EX'S LIVE IN TEXAS

Words and Music by LYNDIA J. SHAFER
and SANGER D. SHAFER

Fdim7
A
love to be.
But all my ex - 's live in
E7
To Coda
Tex - as.
(1-2) And that's why I hang my hat in Ten - nes -
(D.S.) There -
A
G♯
A
see.
Ro - san - na's down in
I re - mem - ber that old
dim.
Bm
Tex - ar - ka - na;
want - ed me to push her broom.
And
Fri - o Riv - er
where I learned to swim.
And it

E7
sweet I - lene's in Ab - i - lene; she for - got I hung the
brings to mind an - oth - er time where I wore my wel - come
A
moon. And Al - li - son in Gal - ves - ton
thin. By tran - scen - den - tal med - i - ta - tion
Bm
some - how lost her san - i - ty.
I go there each night.
B7
And Dim - ples who now
But I al - ways come back
E7
lives in Tem - ple's got the law look - in' for me.
to my - self long be - fore day - light.
cresc.
1
2
D.S. al Coda

CODA
E
A
fore I re - side in Ten - nes - see.
D
D♯
E
D
D♯
Some folks think I'm hid - ing.
E
D
D♯
E
It's been ru - mored that I died.
But I'm a - live and well
A
D6
D♯dim7
A/E
A6/9
in Ten - nes - see.

ALL THE GOLD IN CALIFORNIA

Words and Music by
LARRY GATLIN

F
B♭
F
for - nia, it don't mat - ter at all where you've played
C
To Coda
C7
F
B♭
before; Cal - i - for - nia's a brand new game.
F
B♭
F
Try - in' to be a he - ro, wind - ing up a ze - ro,
B♭/F
F
C
can scar a man for - ev - er right down to your soul.

C7
F
Bb
F
Liv - ing in the spot - light
can kill a man out - right,
Bb
F
C
C7
F
Bb
'cause ev - 'ry - thing that glit - ters
is not gold.
F
D.S. al Coda
And all the
CODA
Bb
game,
Eb
Bb
F
a brand new game.

AUTUMN IN NEW YORK

Words and Music by
VERNON DUKE

Bbm7 Eb9 Ab
4fr
pose of my rose col - ored chat - tels and pre -
Bb7 Eb7#5(b9) Cm7b5 C7sus C7
5fr
pare for my share of ad - ven - tures and bat - tles.
F Gm7b5 F6/9 Gm7b5
5fr 5fr
Here on my twen - ty - sev - enth floor, look - ing down on the cit - y I
Db7 C7#5 G+/F Gb+/C F+ C7#5
4fr
hate and a - dore!

Liltingly and Freely
Gm7
Am7
B♭6
C7
C7♯5
3fr
mf
Au - tumn in New York, why does it seem so in - vit - ing?
Au - tumn in New York, the gleam - ing roof - tops at sun - down.
F
Dm7
Am7
D7♭9(♯11)
D9♯11
4fr
Au - tumn in New York, it spells the thrill of first night - ing.
Au - tumn in New York, it lifts you up when you're run - down.
Am7♭5
D7
Glit - ter - ing crowds and shim - mer - ing clouds in can - yons of steel,
Jad - ed rou - és and gay di - vorc - ees who lunch at the Ritz,
B♭m7
E♭7
A♭maj7

Dm7♭5 Cm/G Cm/D G7♯5
they're mak - ing me feel I'm
will tell you that "it's di -
C C7 C7♯5 Gm7 Am7
home. It's au - tumn in New York
vine!" This au - tumn in New York
B♭6 C7 C7♯5 F Dm7 Am7 D9♯11 D♭9
that brings the prom - ise of new love;
trans - forms the slums in - to May - fair;
Cm7 Dm7 E♭m7 F7
Au - tumn in New York is of - ten min - gled with
Au - tumn in New York, you'll need no cas - tles in

B♭m7
G♭/B♭
B♭m6
Fm
C7♯5
C7
pain.
Spain.
Dream-ers with emp - ty
Lov - ers that bless the
Fm
A♭7
A♭7♯5
D♭
A♭7
A♭7♯5
D♭
D♭9
hands may sigh for ex - o - tic lands; It's
dark on bench - es in Cen - tral Park greet
Gm7
Am7
B♭m6
C7sus♭9
C7♭9
Fm
Au - tumn in New York, it's good to live it a - gain.
Au - tumn in New York; it's good to live it a -
C7
Fm
E♭9
Fm6
gain.
p

ALLEGHENY MOON

Words and Music by DICK MANNING
and AL HOFFMAN

C7+5
F
C7+5
shine, shine, shine High a - mong the
F
stars, so bright a - bove, the mag - ic of your lamp of love can
F+
Bb
D7
Gm
make him (her) mine Al - le - ghe - ny Moon, it's up to
Bbm6
F
E
F7
D7
D7+5
Gm
C9
C7
you, please see what you can do For me and for my one and on - ly
F
Bdim
Gm7
C7+5
2
F
F6
love! Al - le - ghe - ny love!

BIG D
from THE MOST HAPPY FELLA

By FRANK LOESSER

C+
Bb7
I mean Big D, lit - tle a, dou - ble l - a - s.
Eb6
Fm7
F#dim
Gm7-5
Bbm
Ebm7-5
Eb7
And that spells Dal - las, My
that spells Dal - las, Where
that spells Dal - las, Just
that spells Dal - las, I
Fm7
F#dim
Eb7
Ab
C7
Db7
C7
dar - lin', dar - lin' Dal - las, Don't it give you pleas - ure to con -
ev - 'ry home's a pal - ace 'Cause the set - tlers set - tle for no
dig a toe in Dal - las And there's oil all o - ver your ad -
mean it with no mal - ice But the rest of Tex - as looks a
F7
Bb7
Eb
Gm7-5
fess That you're from Big D? My, oh
less Hoo - ray for Big D, My, oh
dress Back home in Big D, My, oh
mess When you're from Big D, My, oh

C7
Bb7
yes.
I mean Big D, lit - tle a, dou - ble l - a,
Eb
Big D, lit - tle a, dou - ble l - a,
Big D, lit - tle
1,2,3
Eb6
Fm7
F#dim
Gm7-5
a, dou - ble l - a - s!
2. And
3. And
4. And
4
F9-5
a, dou - ble l - a - s!

CALIFORNIA GIRLS

Words and Music by BRIAN WILSON
and MIKE LOVE

Bb
Ab/Bb
Mid - west farm - ers' daugh - ters real - ly make you feel al -
been all a - round this great big world, and I've seen all kinds of
Eb
right, and north - ern girls with the way they kiss, they keep their
girls, But I could - n't wait to get back in the states, back to the
F7
Bb
boy - friends warm at night.
cut - est girls in the world.
I wish they all could be
Cm7
Ab
Bbm
Cal - i - for - nia, I wish they all could be Cal - i - for - nia, I

G♭
A♭m
1
B♭
wish they all could be Cal - i - for - nia girls.
2
The girls.
L.H.
I wish they all could be
E♭
Repeat and Fade
Cal - i - for - nia, I wish they all could be Cal - i - for - nia, I

BLUE HAWAII

from the Paramount Picture WAIKIKI WEDDING

Words and Music by LEO ROBIN
and RALPH RAINGER

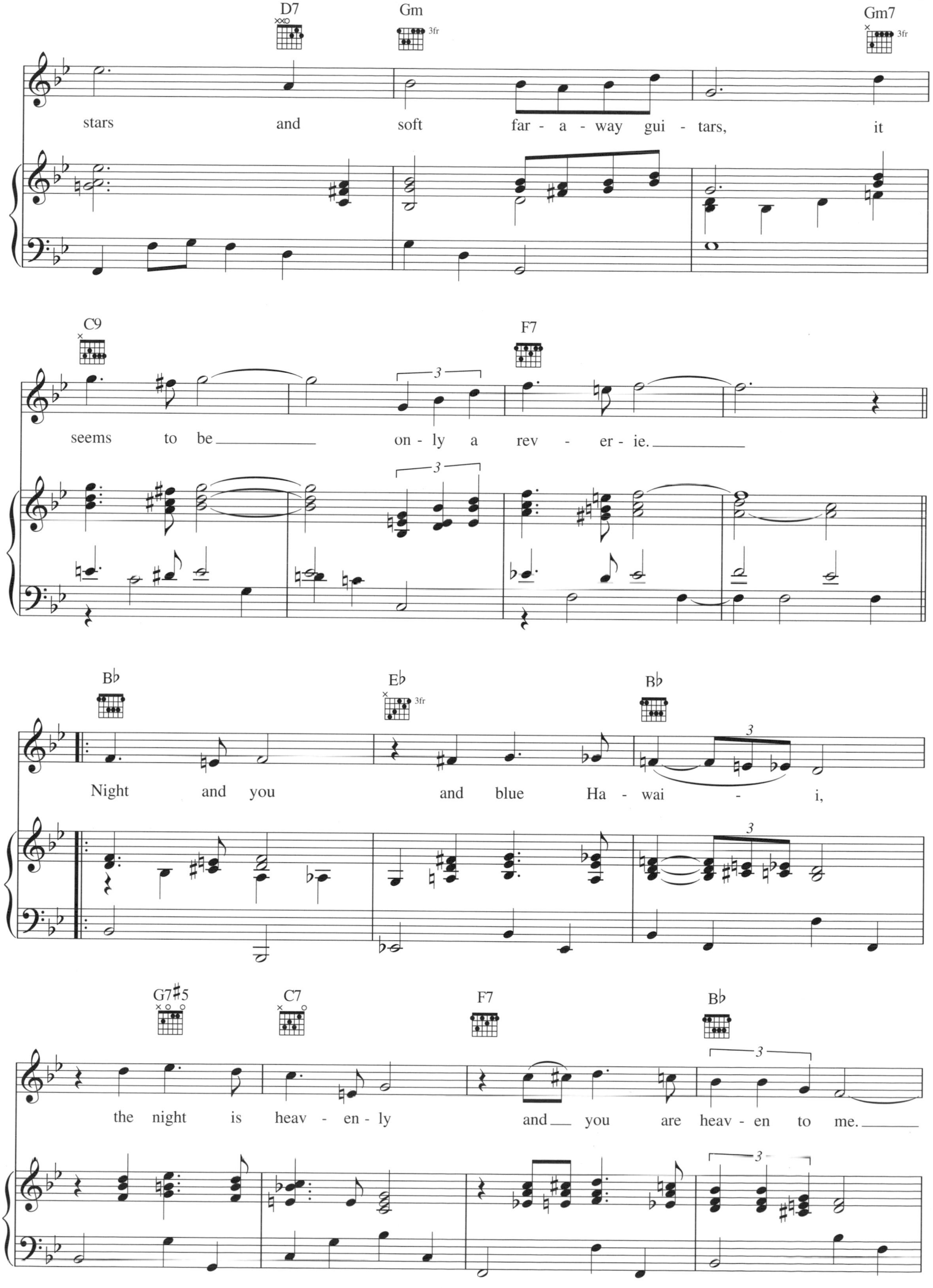

D7 Gm Gm7

stars and soft far - a - way gui - tars, it

C9 F7

seems to be ______ on - ly a rev - er - ie. ______

B♭ E♭ B♭

Night and you and blue Ha - wai - i,

G7♯5 C7 F7 B♭

the night is heav - en - ly and __ you are heav - en to me. ______

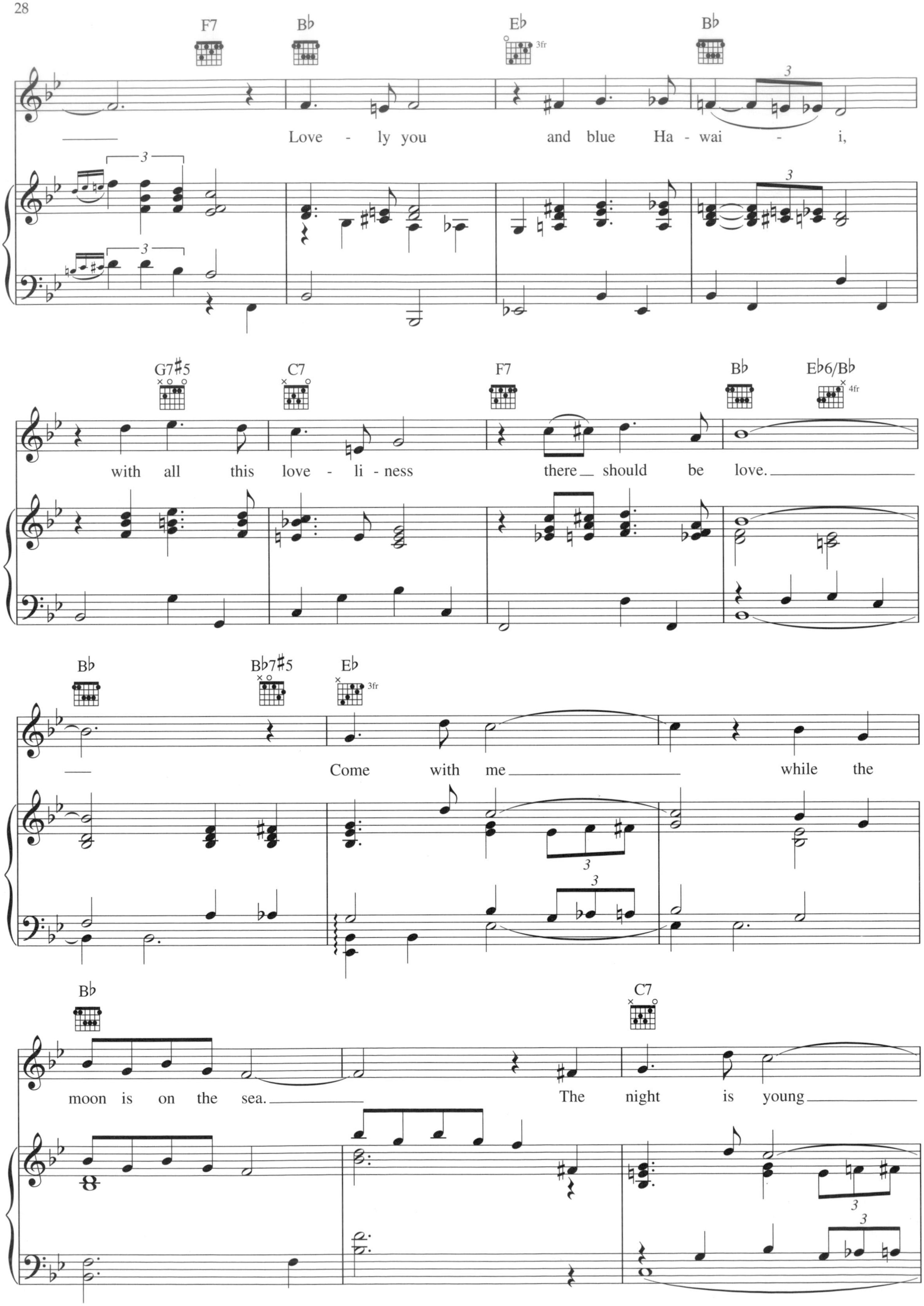
F7
B♭
E♭
3fr
B♭
Love - ly you and blue Ha - wai - i,
G7♯5
C7
F7
B♭
E♭6/B♭
4fr
with all this love - li - ness there should be love.
B♭
B♭7♯5
E♭
3fr
Come with me while the
B♭
C7
moon is on the sea. The night is young

Cm7/F
F7
F7♭9
and so are we.
B♭
E♭
3fr
B♭
Dreams come true in blue Ha - wai - i
G7♯5
C7
F7
and mine could all come true this mag - ic
B♭
E♭/B♭
6fr
1 B♭
F7
2 B♭
night of nights with you.
you.

BLUE MOON OF KENTUCKY

Words and Music by
BILL MONROE

G G7 C
moon keep on a - shin - in' bright you're gon - na bring - a me back - a my
Cm6 G B♭dim D7 G
ba - by to - night; blue moon keep a - shin - in' bright!
D7 G G7 C7
I said blue moon of Ken - tuck - y, to keep on shin - ing,
G D7
shine on the one that's gone and left me blue.

G
G7
I said blue moon of Ken - tuck - y to keep on
C7
G
shin - ing,
shine on the one that's
D7
G
G7
gone and left me blue.
Well, it was
C
C7
G
G7
on one moon - light night,
stars shin - in' bright,

C
C7
G
whis - per on high
love said good -
D7
G
G7
C7
bye; blue moon of Ken - tuck - y, keep on shin - ing,
G
B♭dim
D7
shine on the one that's gone and left me blue.
1
G
A7
D7
I said blue
2
G
G/B
C7
C♯dim
G6

THE BOY FROM NEW YORK CITY

Words and Music by JOHN TAYLOR
and GEORGE DAVIS

Moderate and very steady

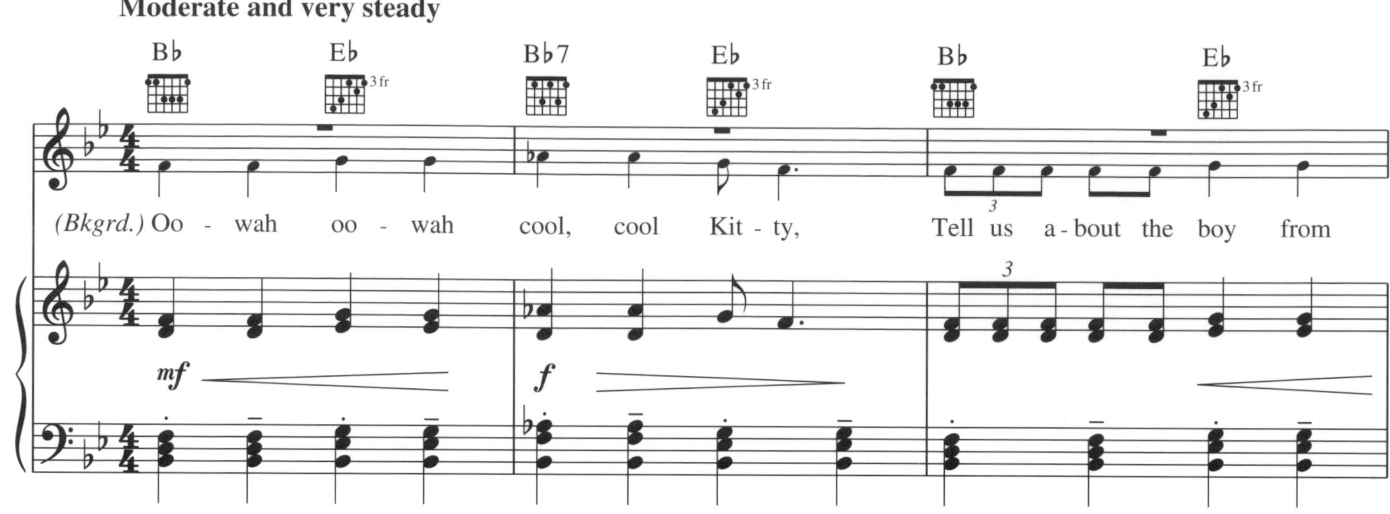

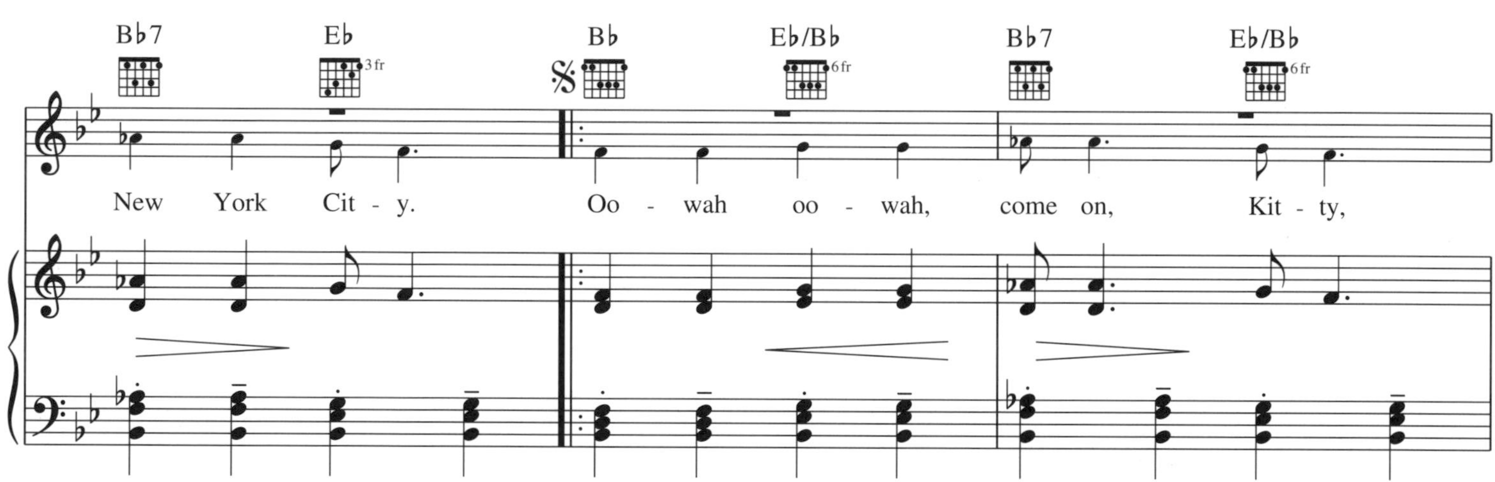

Bb7 Eb/Bb Bb Eb/Bb Bb7 Eb/Bb Bb Eb/Bb
6fr
3
He's real-ly fine. Some day I hope to
and he's no clown. He has the fin - est pent-house I've
and make ro - mance, and that's when I fell in

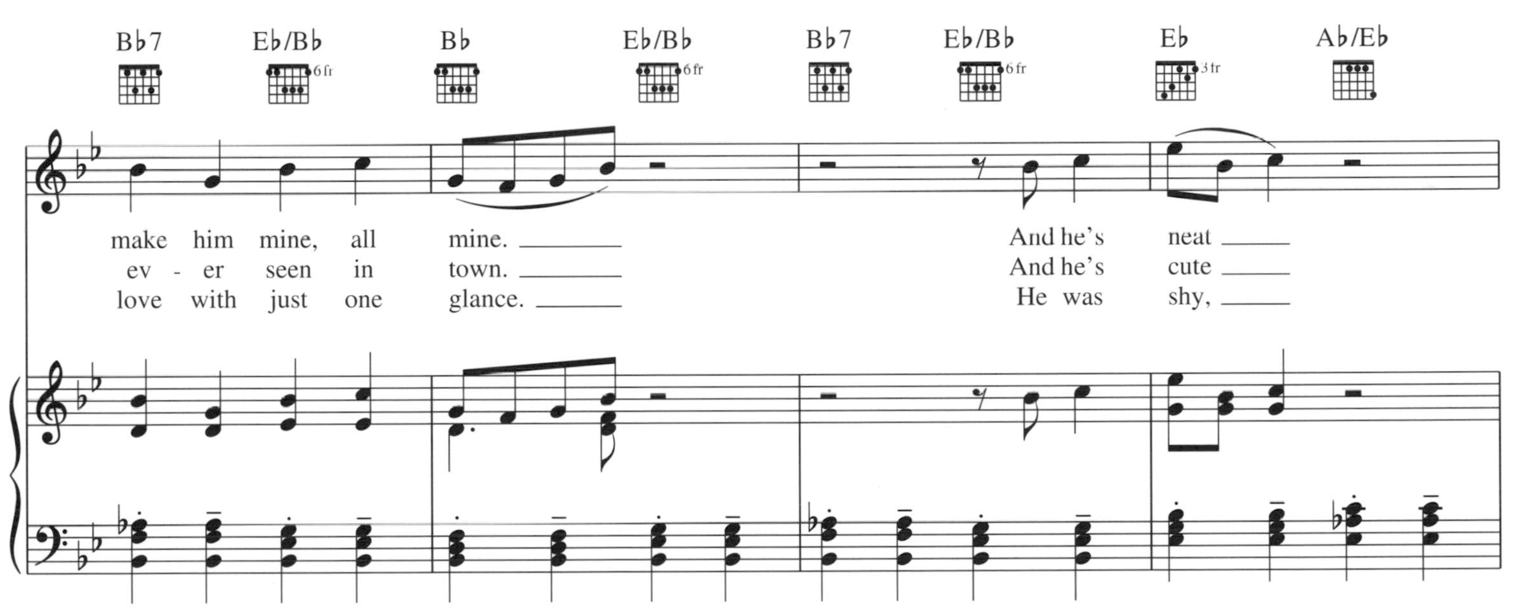
Bb7 Eb/Bb Bb Eb/Bb Bb7 Eb/Bb Eb Ab/Eb
6fr
3fr
make him mine, all mine. And he's neat
ev - er seen in town. And he's cute
love with just one glance. He was shy,

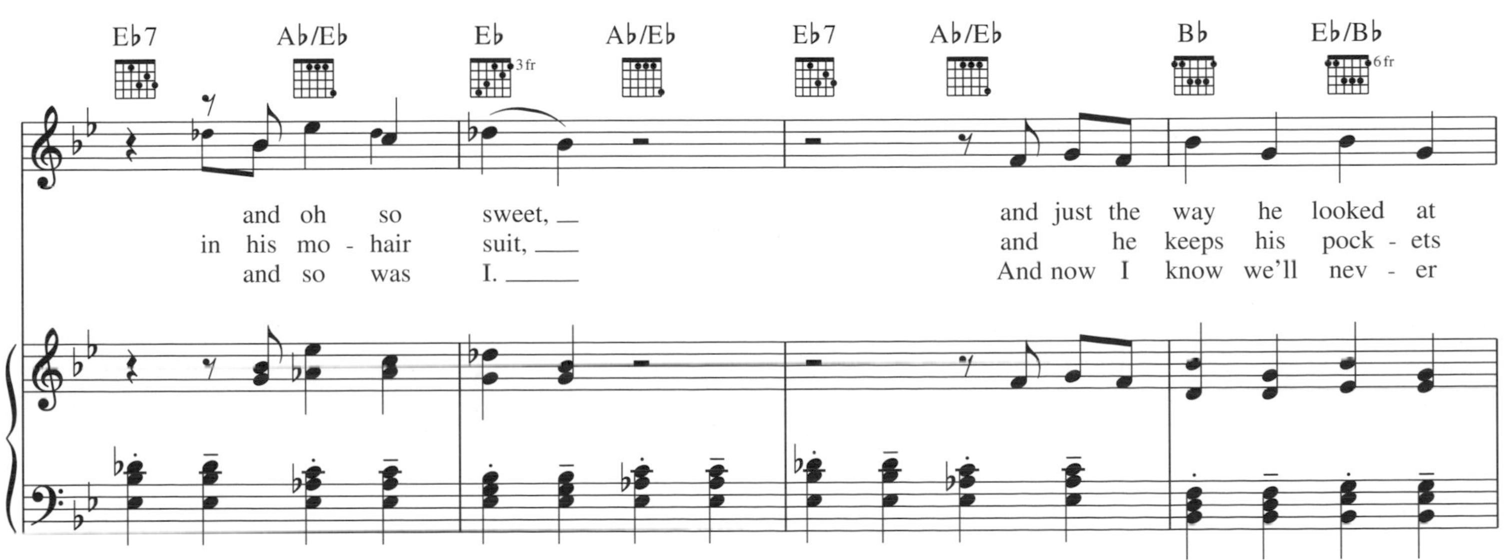
Eb7 Ab/Eb Eb Ab/Eb Eb7 Ab/Eb Bb Eb/Bb
3fr
6fr
and oh so sweet, and just the way he looked at
in his mo - hair suit, and he keeps his pock - ets
and so was I. And now I know we'll nev - er

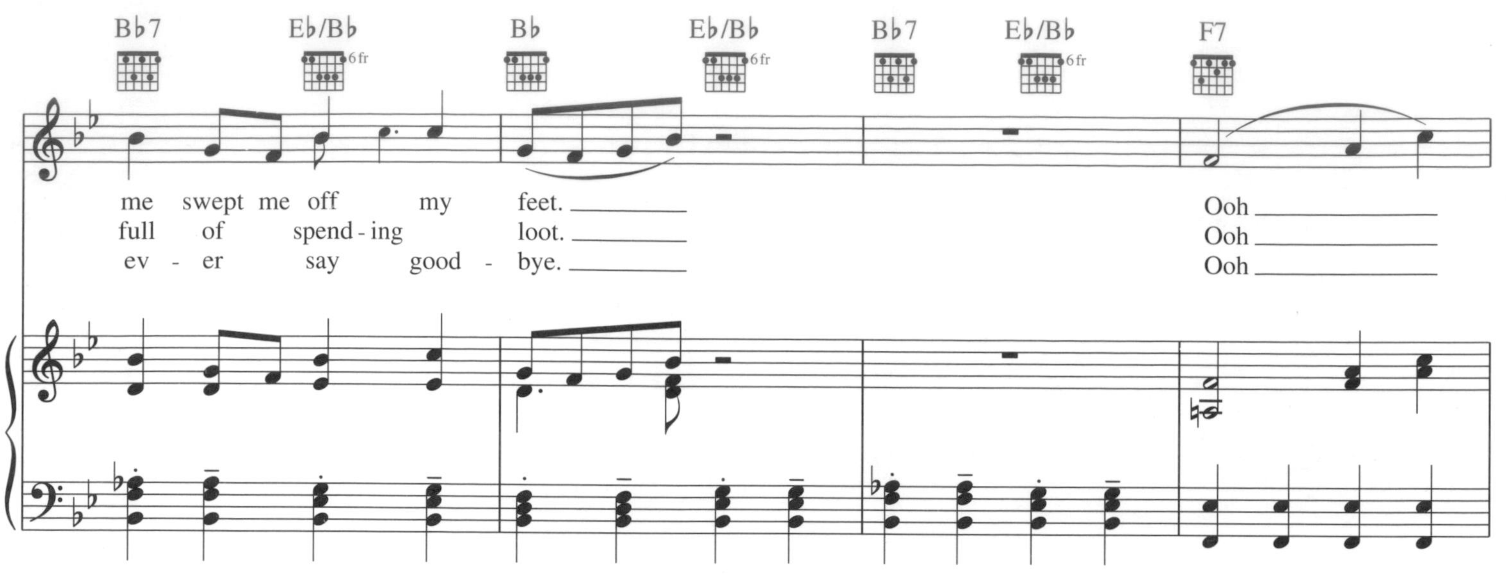
Bb7
Eb/Bb
6fr
Bb
Eb/Bb
6fr
Bb7
Eb/Bb
6fr
F7
me swept me off my feet.
full of spend - ing loot.
ev - er say good - bye.
Ooh
Ooh
Ooh

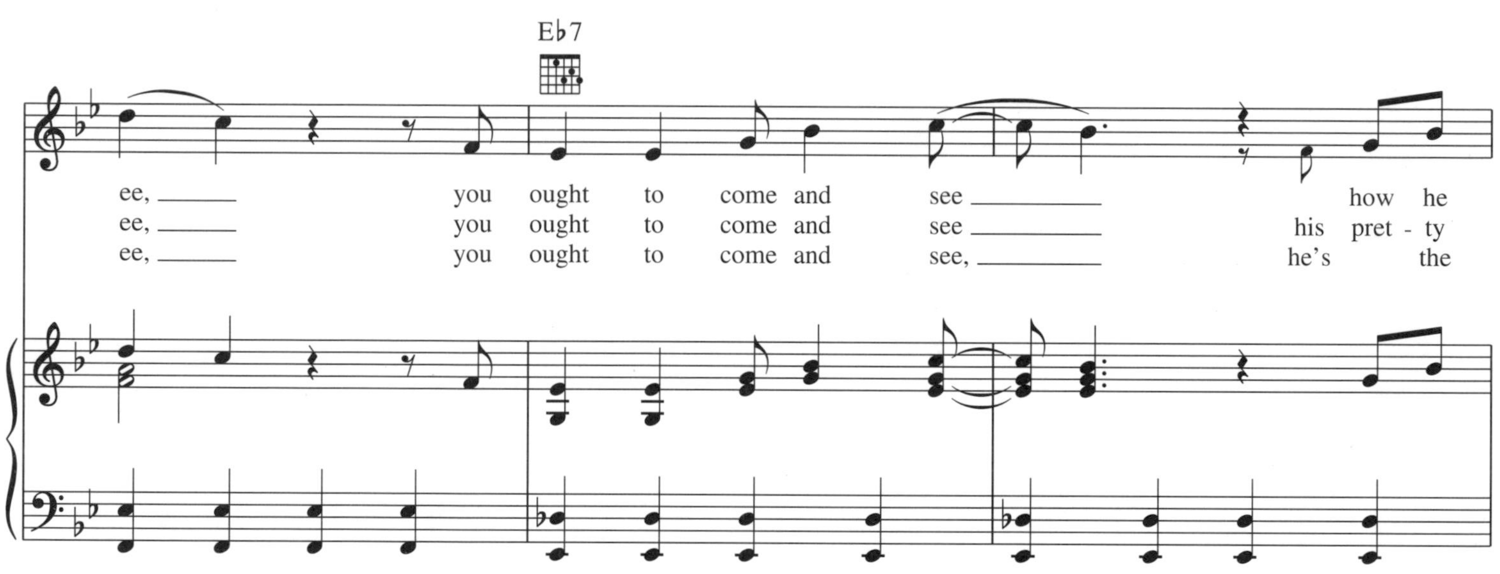
Eb7
ee, you ought to come and see how he
ee, you ought to come and see his pret - ty
ee, you ought to come and see, he's the

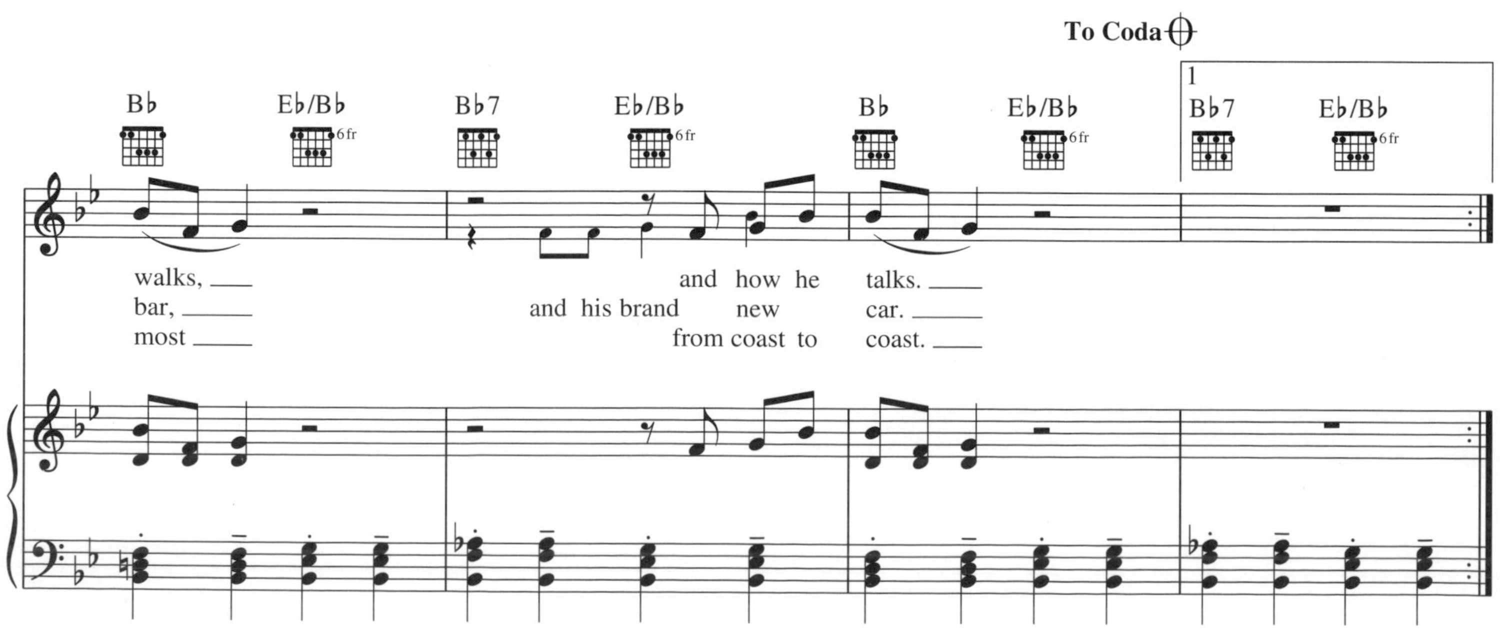
To Coda
Bb
Eb/Bb
6fr
Bb7
Eb/Bb
6fr
Bb
Eb/Bb
6fr
1
Bb7
Eb/Bb
6fr
walks, and how he talks.
bar, and his brand new car.
most from coast to coast.

2
Bb7
Eb/Bb
6fr
Eb
3fr
Ab/Eb
Eb7
Ab/Eb
Bb
Eb/Bb
6fr
Ev - 'ry time he says he loves me, chills run down my
Bb7
Eb/Bb
6fr
Eb
3fr
Ab/Eb
Eb7
Ab/Eb
C7
spine. Ev - 'ry time he wants to kiss me, ooh, he makes me feel so
F7
D.S. al Coda
fine, yeah!
CODA
Bb7
Eb/Bb
6fr
Bb
Eb/Bb
6fr
Oo - wah oo - wah,
(lead vocal ad lib.)
Repeat and Fade
Bb7
Eb/Bb
6fr
Bb
Eb/Bb
6fr
Bb7
Eb/Bb
6fr
come on, Kit - ty, tell us a - bout the boy from New York Cit - y.
3

BY THE TIME I GET TO PHOENIX

Words and Music by
JIMMY WEBB

1
Fm7
Db
Bb7
2
Fm7
left that girl so man-y times be - fore.
By the wall,
Db
Bb7
D.S. al Coda
that's all.
By the
CODA
Fm7
time and time
Bb7
Ebmaj7
Abmaj7
Fm
G
I've tried to tell her so;
she just did-n't know
I would real-ly
C
Bb
C
Bb
C
go.

CALIFORNIA, HERE I COME

Words and Music by AL JOLSON, B.G. DeSYLVA and JOSEPH MEYER

Em7 A7 Am7 Em C7 B7
west - ward, know - ing that's the place I love the best of
heart grow fond - er," of the good old place you leave be -
Em G7 G11/A Gm7♭5/B♭ G7/B
all. Cal - i - for - nia,
hind. When you've hit the
F/C C G7 G11/A Gm7♭5/B♭ G7/B
I've been blue, since I've been a -
train a while, seems you rare - ly
F/C C B7 B7♯5 B7 Em
way from you. I can't
see a smile; that's why

Em(maj7)
Em7
A7
Am7
Em
wait 'til I get go - ing. E - ven now I'm
I must fly out yon - der, where a frown is
C7
B7
Em
G7
start - ing in to call, oh,
might - y hard to find! Oh,
C
C+/E
F
Cal - i - for - nia, here I come,
G7
Dm7/A
A♯dim7
G7/B
C
right back where I start - ed from,

C/E
D♯dim
G7/D
G7
where bow - ers of flow - ers bloom in the sun.
C/E
D♯dim
Each morn - ing, at dawn - ing,
G7/D
N.C.
bird - ies sing and ev - 'ry - thing. A sun - kissed
C
C+/E
F
miss said "Don't be late."

G7
Dm7/A
A♯dim7
G7/B
Em7
A7
Gm6/B♭
A7
That's why I can hard - ly wait.
Dm
A7/E
Dm/F
F♯dim
C/G
E7/G♯
Am
O - pen up that Gold - en Gate; Cal - i -
D7
F/G
G7
1
C
D♯dim7
for - nia, here I come!
Dm7
G+
3fr
2
C
F7
C
come!

CAROLINA IN MY MIND

Words and Music by
JAMES TAYLOR

Dm
B♭
Dm
G7
C7
friend of mine _ to hit me from _ be - hind? _ And I'm
F
Gm7
3 fr
C7sus
F
Gm
3 fr
C7sus
gone to Car - o - li - na in _ my mind. _
F
E♭
3 fr
B♭
Kar - in she's _ a sil - ver sun, _ you'd best walk her a - way and
Dark and si - lent late last night, _ I think I might have heard the high - way
C
Dm
B♭
C
watch it shine. _ Watch her watch _ the morn-ing come. _
call. _ Geese in flight _ and _ dogs that bite. _

Gm7
3 fr
C7
B♭
F
Dm7
G7
A sil - ver tear ap - pear - ing now I'm cry - ing
And signs that might be o - mens say I'm go - ing,
B♭
C7
F
Gm7
3 fr
C7sus
To Coda
ain't I?
go - ing.
I'm gone to Car - o - li - na in my mind.
F
E♭
3 fr
There ain't no doubt no one's mind that love's
B♭
C
Dm
the fin - est thing a - round.
Whis - per some -

Bb
C7sus
C7
Bb
- thing soft and kind.
And hey, babe, the
F
Dm7
G7
Bb
C7
sky's on fire, I'm dy - ing, ain't I?
I'm
F
Gm7
3 fr
C7sus
F
D.S. al Coda
gone to Car - o - li - na in my mind.
CODA
F
Bb
Now with a ho - ly host of

F
Dm7
oth - ers stand - ing 'round me no,
Am
Gm7
3 fr
C7
Still I'm on the dark side of the moon. And it
E♭
3 fr
B♭
F
seems like it goes on like this for - ev - er,
E♭
3 fr
Gm7
3 fr
you must for - give me.

Gm7/C
F
B♭
If it's up in,
In my mind I'm gone to Car - o - li -
Gm7
3 fr
C7
B♭
C7
- na.
Can't you see the sun - shine? And
Gm7
3 fr
C7
F
can't you just feel the moon - shine?
And ain't it just like a
Dm
B♭
Dm
G7
C7
friend of mine to hit me from be - hind?
And I'm

1
F
Gm7
3 fr
C7sus
F
gone to Car - o - li - na in my mind.
Gm
3 fr
C7sus
2
F
B♭
F/A
gone to Car - o - li - na
Gm7
3 fr
Gm7/C
F
in my mind.
Gm7
3 fr
G♭maj7
F

CHICAGO
(That Toddlin' Town)

Words and Music by
FRED FISHER

C D7 E♭7
Bet your bot - tom dol - lar you lose the blues in Chi - ca - go, Chi -
Am7 D7 C♯dim7 Dm7 G9 Dm7 G9 Fdim7
ca - go. The folks who vis - it all wan - na set - tle
Em7 E♭9 Dm7 G7sus C Dm7 Em7 A7
down. On State Street, that great street, I
Dm7 G7 Dm7 G7 A7♯5 Dm7 G7
just wan - na say, (just wan - na say,) they do things they

Bm7
E7
Am
A7
don't do on Broad - way.
Say,
F
B♭9
C/G
G7♯5
you'll have the time, the time of your life.
Bring all your friends, your kids
C/G
E♭dim7
G7
A♭7
G7
and your wife to Chi - ca - go,
Chi - ca - go, my home town.
1
C Em7
E♭9
Dm7
G7sus
Chi -
2
C Em7
E♭m6
Dm7 D♭maj7 Cmaj7

DO YOU KNOW WHAT IT MEANS TO MISS NEW ORLEANS

Lyric by EDDIE DE LANGE
Music by LOUIS ALTER

Cm/E♭
D♭9
Cm
A♭9
here's the mat - ter,
Here's the thing that's real - ly wrong with
Fm6/G
G7
C
G+
me: Do you know what it means to
C
Am
Em
Am
miss New Or - leans
And miss it each night and
D9
F
F♯dim
day? I know I'm not wrong, the

C
A7
Dm
A♭7
feel - in's get - tin' strong - er The long - er I stay a - way
G7
C
G+
Miss the moss - cov - ered vines, the
C
Am
Em
Am
tall sug - ar pines Where mock - in' - birds used to
D9
F
F♯dim
C
A7
sing And I'd like to see the la - zy Mis - sis - sip - pi A

Dm
G7
G+
C
Dm
Cdim
C
hur - ry - in' in - to spring. The
Bbm7
Eb9
Eb7
Ab
Adim
Bbm7
Eb9
Eb7
moon - light on the bay - ou A Cre - ole tune that fills the
Ab
Am7
D9
D7
air; I dream a - bout mag -
G
F#7
Em
Am7
D9
nol - ias in June And soon I'm wish - in' that I was there.

G9 Fm6 G7 C G+ C Am
Do you know what it means _ to miss New Or - leans _ When
Em Am D9
that's where you left ___ your heart? And
F F♯dim C A+ A7
there's some - thing more: ___ I miss the one I care for
D9 G7♭9 1 C A♭9 G7 2 C
More than I miss _ New Or - leans. Do you leans.

CLEVELAND ROCKS

Theme from THE DREW CAREY SHOW

Words and Music by
IAN HUNTER

D♭5
4fr
All the lit - tle chicks with the crim - son lips go,
A♭5
4fr
D♭5
4fr
"Cleve - land rocks, Cleve - land rocks." She's liv - in' in sin with a
A♭
4fr
B♭/A♭
safe - ty pin go - in', "Cleve - land rocks, Cleve - land rocks,
D♭/A♭
4fr
A♭5
4fr
A♭
4fr
Cleve - land rocks."
Spoken: Ohio.

DEEP IN THE HEART OF TEXAS

Words by JUNE HERSHEY
Music by DON SWANDER

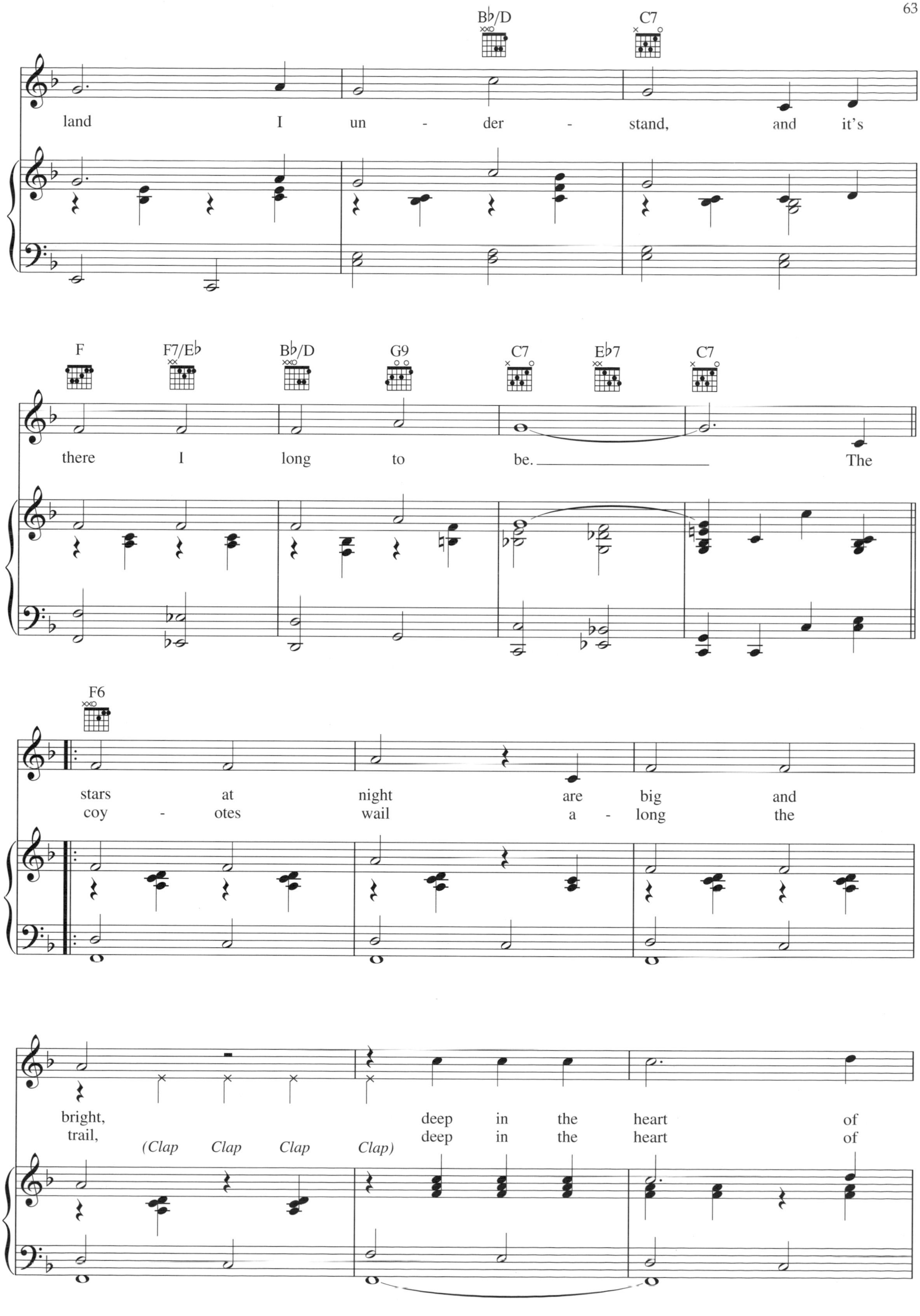

B♭/D C7

land I un - der - stand, and it's

F F7/E♭ B♭/D G9 C7 E♭7 C7

there I long to be. The

F6

stars at night are big and
coy - otes wail a - long the

bright, deep in the heart of
trail, deep in the heart of
(Clap Clap Clap Clap)

C7
Tex - as; The prai - rie
Tex - as; The rab - bits
sky is wide and high,
rush a - round the brush,
(Clap Clap Clap
Clap)
deep in the heart of Tex - as.
deep in the heart of Tex - as.
F
F6
The sage in bloom is like per -
The cow - boys cry, "Ki - yip - pee -

C7
fume, deep in the heart of Tex - as;
yi," deep in the heart of Tex - as;
(Clap Clap Clap Clap)
Re - minds me of the
The dog - ies bawl, and
one I love, deep in the heart of
bawl and bawl, deep in the heart of
(Clap Clap Clap Clap)
1 F Gm7 C7
2 F B♭6 F
Tex - as. The
Tex - as.
8vb

DO YOU KNOW THE WAY TO SAN JOSE

Lyric by HAL DAVID
Music by BURT BACHARACH

B♭6
F
C7sus
way to San _ Jo - se? I'm go - ing back to find some _ peace of
raised in San _ Jo - se. I'm go - ing back to find some _ peace of
C7
Am7
Dm7
mind in San _ Jo - se. L. A. is a great _ big free - way.
mind in San _ Jo - se. Fame and for - tune is _ a mag - net.
Am7
Dm7
Am
Put a hun - dred down _ and buy _ a car. _
It can pull you far _ a - way _ from home. _
F♯m7♭5
4 fr
Gm7/F
C/E
In a week may - be two, they'll make _ you a star.
With a dream in your heart you're nev - er a - lone.

Gm7
3 fr
C
N.C.
Weeks turn in - to years. How quick _ they pass, ____ and all the stars
Dreams turn in - to dust and blow _ a - way, ____ and there you are
___ that nev - er were ___ are park - ing cars ___ and pump - ing gas. ___
___ with - out a friend. _ You pack your car ____ and ride ___ a - way. _
mp
1
2
F
I've got lots of
B♭6
Fmaj7
friends in San ___ Jo - se.

F
B♭6
Fmaj7
Do you know the way to San _ Jo - se?
F
B♭6
Can't wait to get back to San _ Jo - se.
Fmaj7
Fmaj7
N.C.
8va bassa
Repeat and Fade

GALVESTON

Words and Music by
JIM WEBB

B♭
Dm/A
Gm7
C
Dm
B♭/C
glow - ing.
She was twen - ty one,
when
flash - in'.
I clean my gun,
and
B♭
B♭/C
I left Gal - ves - ton.
dream of Gal - ves - ton.
1
F
B♭
C
2
F
B♭
F
A♭
B♭
I still see her stand - ing by the wa -
A♭
B♭
Cm
- ter,
stand - ing there

A♭
4 fr
Fm
B♭7
looking out to sea.
And is she waiting there for
E♭
3fr
Gm
3fr
Cm
3fr
D♭
me,
on the beach where we used to run?
B♭
C
F
Galveston, oh! Galveston,
Fmaj7
F7
I am so afraid of

B♭
Dm/A
Gm7
3fr
C
F
dy - ing,
be - fore I dry
the tears she's
B♭
Dm/A
Gm7
3fr
C
Dm
F/C
cry - ing,
be - fore I watch
your sea birds
B♭
Am
Gm7
3fr
C
fly - ing in the sun
at Gal - ves - ton,
D
C
D
at Gal - ves - ton.

GEORGIA ON MY MIND

Words by STUART GORRELL
Music by HOAGY CARMICHAEL

A7
D7
D7♯5
D7
G9
C7
blos - soms fall and all the world's a song,
F
A7♯5
A7/D
Dm
G7
Edim7
C13
2fr
F
I'll go back to Geor - gia 'cause that's where I be - long.
F
A7
Dm
Geor - gia,
Geor - gia,
the whole day
Gm
3fr
B♭m
F
E7
Gm
3fr
G9
C7
F
F♯dim
through. Just an old sweet song keeps Geor - gia on my mind.

Gm7
C7♯5
F
A7
(Geor - gia on my mind.)
Geor - gia,
Geor - gia,
Dm
Gm
B♭m
F
E7
a song of you
comes as sweet and clear as
Gm
G9
C13
F
E♭9
F
A7
Dm
Gm6
moon - light through the pines.
Oth - er arms reach
Dm
B♭7
Dm
Gm6
Dm7
G7
out to me;
Oth - er eyes smile ten - der - ly;

Dm Gm6 Dm7 E7 Am F#dim Fm6
Still in peace - ful dreams I see the road leads back to
Dm C7 F A7 Dm
you. Geor - gia, Geor - gia, no peace I
Gm B♭m F E7 Gm G9 C13
find. Just an old sweet song keeps Geor - gia on my
1
F Dm Gm7 C13 C7#5
mind.
2
F B♭6/9 C7#5 F6
mind.
rit.

HARLEM NOCTURNE

Words by DICK ROGERS
Music by EARLE HAGEN

Cm7
3fr
E♭7
D7
the dark - ness is taunt - ing me.
Gm6
3fr
N.C.
Gm6
3fr
Oh! what a sad re - frain,
Cm6
a noc - turne born in Har - lem.
Cm7
3fr
E♭7
D7
That mel - an - chol - y strain
for - ev - er is haunt - ing me.

Gm6
C9
Gm6
Gb9
F9
Bb7
Fm7
Bb7
Fm7
The mel - o - dy clings a - round my heart strings, it
Bb7
Fm7
Bb7
B7
Bb7
won't let me go when I'm lone - ly. I
Eb7
Bbm7
Eb7
Bbm7
hear it in dreams and some - how it seems it

N.C.
makes me weep and I can't sleep. An
F7
Bb7
Fm7
in - di - go tune, it sings to the moon the lone-some re - frain of a
B7
Eb7
Bbm7
lov - er. The mel - o - dy sighs, it laughs and it cries a
moan in blue that wails the long night

Gm6
D7♯5
Gm6
N.C.
Gm6
thru. Tho' with the dawn it's gone,
Cm6
the mel - o - dy lives ev - er for lone - ly hearts to learn
Cm7
E♭7
D7
Gm6
Cm6
of love in a Har - lem Noc - turne.
Gm6
Cm6
Gm
D7
Gm(add9)
C13
Gm(add9)
molto rit.

HAWAIIAN LOVE CALL

Written by ALULI IRMGARD FARDEN

Eb Cm7 Cm G+ Cm7 F7 E7 F7
i - po with an a - lo - ha that is
Cm7 F7 Bb
Tacet
pre - cious sweet. My dear - est
Fm Bb7 Fm Eb
one it's you I want.
Tacet
Gm C7
My pre - cious one sweet voice

Cm7
F7
Tacet
B♭
F7
of love. Lis - ten to my call,
B♭
B♭+
E♭
Cm7
Cm
G+
Cm7
my ku - u i - po Then an - swer
F7
E7
F7
Cm7
F7
1 B♭
B♭6
Gdim
ten - der - ly that you'll be mine.
(rit. last time)
Cm7
F7
Tacet
2 G♭6
B♭6
Lis - ten to my mine.
slowly

THE HAWAIIAN WEDDING SONG

(Ke Kali Nei Au)

English Lyrics by AL HOFFMAN and DICK MANNING
Hawaiian Lyrics and Music by CHARLES E. KING

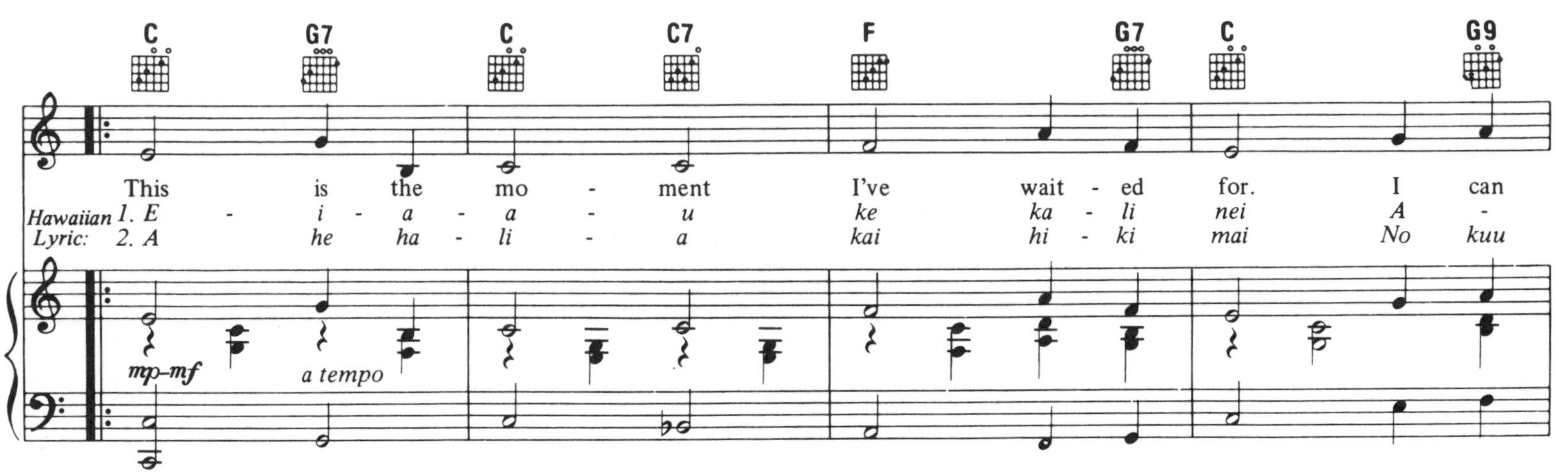

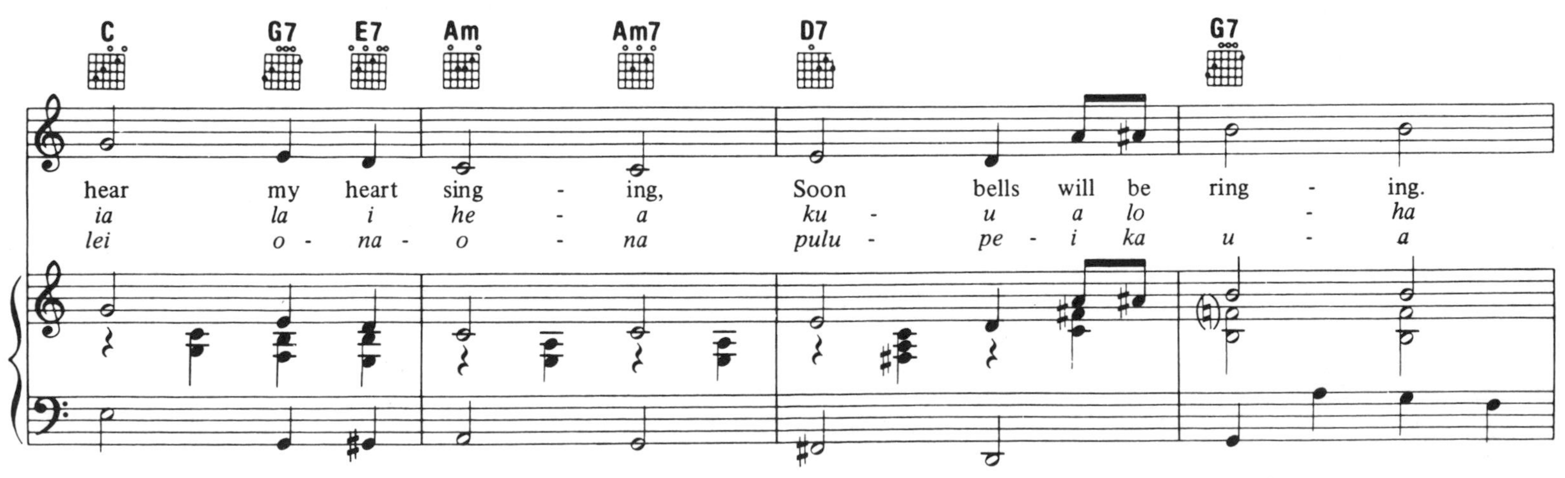

C Cdim D7 G7 C
This is the mo - ment of sweet "A lo - ha,"
E - i - a a - u ke hu - li ne - i
Au - he - a o - e kai - ini a lo - ko
C G9 G7
I will love you long - er than for - ev - er, Prom - ise me that you will leave me
A lo - a - a o - e e ka i - po Ma - ha ka i - i - ni a ka
Na lo - ko a - e ka ma - na o Hu - 'e la - ni a - na i kuu
C G+ C A7 D7 G7
nev - er. Here and now, dear, All my love I
pu - u - wai. U - a si - la pa - a ia me
ki - no. Ku - u pu - a ku - u lei ona
C Cdim G9
vow, dear, Prom - ise me that you will leave me nev - er,
o - e Ko a - lo - ha ma - ka - mae e i - po
o - na A'u i kui a la - wa i - a - ne - i

G7 C F D7 G7 C A7 D7 G7 C A7 D7 G7
I will love you long - er than for - ev - er. Now that we are one, Clouds won't hide the sun. Blue skies of Ha - wai - i smile on this, our wed - ding day. I do love you with all my heart.
Ka - 'u ia e le - i a - e ne - i la Nou no ka i - ini A nou wa - le no A o ko a - lo - ha ka'u e hi - i - po - i mau Na'u oe e lei na'u oe e lei.
Me ke a - la pu - a pi - ka - ke A o oe kuu pua kuu pua lei le - hua A'u e li - 'a ma - u nei hoo - paa ia iho kea - loha. He lei, oe na'u, he lei oe na'u.
1 C G7
2 C
heart.
lei.
na'u.
mf

I LEFT MY HEART IN SAN FRANCISCO

Words by DOUGLASS CROSS
Music by GEORGE CORY

D7♭9
4fr
Gm
3fr
Gm(maj7)
3fr
C9sus
that was Rome is of an-
C9
F9sus
Freely
F9
Cm7♭5
oth - er day. I've been ter - ri - bly a -
rit.
Gm7♭5
5fr
G♭9
3fr
With a slow, steady beat
F/C
lone and for - got - ten in Man - hat - tan. I'm go - ing
D7/C
C9sus
C9
F9sus
Fdim7
home to my cit - y by the bay.

F9
Cm7
3fr
C♯dim7
B♭maj9
C♯dim7
I left my heart in San Fran -
Cm7
3fr
F9sus
cis - co.
High on a hill,
F7
B♭maj7
Cm7
3fr
B♭maj7
Cm7
3fr
C♯dim7
it calls to me.
To be where
B♭maj7
B♭m6
6fr
Am/C
lit - tle ca-ble cars
climb half-way to the stars!
3

Am7 D7♭9 Gm7 C9 C7♭9

The morn - ing fog may chill the

F9sus F9 Bdim7 Cm7 F7 C♯dim7 B♭maj9

air; I don't care! My love waits there

C♯dim7 Cm7

in San Fran - cis - co, a - bove the

F9 E♭6/G F7/A E♭/G E♭6 D C/E

blue and wind - y sea.

D7/F♯
D7
G7♯5
G9
F/A
G7/B
When I come home to you, San Fran -
C9sus
Gm7
C9
B9
C9
F9sus
cis - co, your gold - en sun will
Cm7
F7♭5(♭9)
1
B♭6
A♭13
B♭6/9
Cm7
C♯dim7
shine for me! I left my
2
B♭6
A♭13
B♭6/9
G♭maj7
B♭6/9
me!
dim. e rit.

INDIANA
(Back Home Again in Indiana)

Words by BALLARD MacDONALD
Music by JAMES F. HANLEY

Am
G#dim7
Am
D7
G
Gdim7
vi - sion fair I see A - gain I seem to
of - ten times I see A scene that's dear to
Am7
D
G
E7
A7
be:
me:
Back home a - gain in In - di - an - a, And it
D7
G
G7
seems that I can see The gleam - ing
C
Gdim
G
can - dle - light still shin - ing bright Thru the

A7
D7
G
E7
syc - a - mores for me, The new mown hay sends all its
A7
D7
D♯dim7
Em
E♭7
fra - grance From the fields I used to roam, When I
G/D
B7
Em
C♯dim7
dream a - bout the moon - light on the Wa - bash, Then I
G/D
D7
1
G
2
G
long for my In - di - an - a home. Back home a - home.
3

IT NEVER RAINS
(In Southern California)

Words and Music by ALBERT HAMMOND
and MICHAEL HAZELWOOD

D
G
- ni - ties
T V breaks and mov - ies rang
Am7
D
G
C6
G
true,
sure rang true.
Seems it
Am7
D
G
nev - er rains in south - ern Cal - i - for - nia,
Am7
D
seems I've of - ten heard that kind of talk be - fore.

G
Am7
D
It nev - er rains in Cal - i - for - nia, But
G
Em
Am7
D
girl, don't they warn ya, it pours, man, it pours.
G
C6
G
Am7
Out of work, I'm out a' my head,
D
G
out of self re - spect, I'm out a' bread. I'm un - der -

Am7
D
G
loved, I'm un - der - fed.
I wan - na go home.
It nev - er
rains in Cal - i - for - nia,
but girl, don't they warn
ya, it pours,
man, it pours.
Em
C6
Will you tell the folks back home
I near - ly

G
Am7
made it, had of - fers but don't
D
G
C
G
Am7
know which one to take. Please don't tell them how you found
D
G
Em
Am7
me, don't tell them how you found me. Give me a break,
D
G
C6
1
G
2
G
give me a break. Seems it

JACKSON

Words and Music by BILLY EDD WHEELER
and JERRY LEIBER

We been talk - in' 'bout Jack -
Play your hand like a lov - er man,
All them wom - en gon - na beg
lead you 'round town like a scol - ded hound
E♭7
E♭6
E♭
A♭/B♭
4fr.
son e - ver since the fire went
make a big fool of your -
me, teach 'em what they don't know
with your tail tucked be - tween your
E♭
A♭
4fr.
out. (He:) I'm goin' to Jack - son,
self. Go on to Jack - son,
how. I'm goin' to Jack - son,
legs. So go on down to Jack - son,
E♭
gon - na mess a - round.
comb your hair.
turn loose my coat.
you big talk - in' man.

Yeah, I'm goin' to
(He:) Got - ta snow ball
I'm goin' to
I'll be wait - in' in
A♭
4fr.
B♭7
Jack - son,
Jack - son.
Jack - son,
Jack - son,
you know I'm
"Good - bye", that's
be - hind my
E♭
plea - sure bound.
(She:) See if I care.
all she wrote.
Ja - pan fan.
1. 2. 3. 4.
5.
(She:) Well,
(He:) When
(She:) When they

KANSAS CITY

Words and Music by JERRY LEIBER and MIKE STOLLER

G7
F7
cra - zy way of lov - in' there and I'm gon - na get me some.
C7
I'm gon - na be
3
C
stand - in' on the cor - ner Twelfth Street and Vine.
pack my clothes, leave at the crack of dawn.
I'm gon - na be
I'm go - in' to

F7
stand - in' on the cor - ner
Twelfth Street and Vine,
pack my clothes,
leave at the crack of dawn.
C
with my
My old
G7
F7
Kan - sas Cit - y ba - by and a bot - tle of Kan - sas Cit - y wine.
la - dy will be sleep - in' an' she won't know where I'm gone.
C7
Well, I
'Cause if I

C
F7
might take a train, I might take a plane, but
stay with that wom - an I know I'm gon - na die, got - ta
C
if I have to walk I'm goin' just the same. I'm go - in' to
find a brand new ba - by and that's the rea - son why I'm go - in' to
F7
Kan - sas Cit - y, Kan - sas Cit - y here I
C
come. They got a

G7
F7
crazy way of lovin' there and I'm gonna get me some.
C7
1
I'm goin' to
2
G7
They got a crazy way of lovin' there and
F7
C7
I'm gonna get me some.

KENTUCKY RAIN

Words and Music by EDDIE RABBITT
and DICK HEARD

Slow (triplet feel)

mf

Slow 4

C G C F

Sev - en lone - ly days and a doz - en towns a - go, I
Showed your pho - to - graph to some old gray beard - ed men Sit - ting

mp-mf

C F C C7 F G

reached out one night and you were gone; Don't know why you'd run, what you're
on a bench out - side a gen - 'ral store; They said, "Yes, _ she's been here," but their

C Am D7

run - nin' to or __ from, All I know is I want to bring you
mem - 'ry was - n't clear, Was it yes - ter - day, no _ wait, the day be -

G7
C
G
C
F
home.
So I'm Walk-ing in the rain,
thumb-ing for a ride,
On this
fore.
Fi-n'ly got a ride
with a preach-er man who asked, "Where you
C
F
C
C7
F
G
lone-ly
Ken-tuck-y
back road,
I've
loved you much too long
and
bound
on such a
dark
aft-er-noon?"
As we drove on thru the rain,
as he
C
Am
D7
my love's
too
strong,
To
let
you go,
nev-er
know-ing
what
went
lis-tened,
I ex-plained,
And he
left
me
with a
prayer
that I'd
find
G7
Fmaj7
D7
C
Bm
wrong.
you.
Ken-tuck-y
rain keeps pour-ing
down,

Em Am G F Em F C Fmaj7
And up a - head's an - oth - er town that I'll go walk - ing thru, _ With the
C Em Am Em C Am F
rain in my shoes, Search - ing for you.
G7 C Em F G7 1 C
In the cold Ken - tuck - y rain, _ In the cold Ken - tuck - y rain.
2 C Em F G7 Repeat and Fade
rain, _ In the cold Ken - tuck - y

LAST TRAIN TO CLARKSVILLE

Words and Music by BOBBY HART
and TOMMY BOYCE

C7
slow.
Oh...
Oh, no, no, no!
Oh, no, no, no!
'Cause I'm
Take the
G7
leav - ing in the morn - ing and I must see you a -
last train to Clarks - ville, now I must hang up the
gain. We'll have one more night to - geth - er 'til the
phone. I can't hear you in this nois - y rail - road

C7
morn - ing brings my train. And I must go.
sta - tion all a - lone I'm feel - in' low.
Oh, no, no, no!
Oh, no, no, no!
D7
And I don't know if I'm ev - er com - ing
G
2nd time D.S. and Fade
home.
Take the

THE LITTLE OLD LADY
(From Pasadena)

Words and Music by DON ALTFELD
and ROGER CHRISTIAN

Moderately, with a beat

C
white gar - de - nias.
nev - er lose her.
four - two - six now.
(Go Gran - ny, go, Gran - ny,
G7
C7
F
go, Gran - ny, go.)
But parked in a rick - et - y
She's gon - na get a tick - et now,
The guys come to race her from
B♭
G
E♭
3fr
C
old gar - age, there's a brand new shin - y su - per stocked Dodge.
soon - er or la - ter, 'cause she can't keep her foot off the ac - cel - er - a - tor.
miles a - round, but she'll give 'em a length, then she'll shut 'em down.
F
And ev - 'ry - bod - y's say - in' that there's no - bod - y mean - er than the

B♭7
lit - tle old la - dy from Pas - a - de - na. She drives real fast and she
F
drives real hard. She's the ter - ror of Col - o - ra - do Bou - le - vard. It's the
A♭
4fr
C7
1, 2
lit - tle old la - dy from Pas - a - de - na!
If you
You'll
3
F
Repeat and Fade
The lit - tle old la - dy from Pas - a - de - na. The

PITTSBURGH, PENNSYLVANIA

Words and Music by
BOB MERRILL

G/D
D7
G
van - ia and I walk up and down 'neath the clock.
Am7
D7
G
Gmaj7/F#
By the pawn - shop on a cor - ner in
G6/E
G/D
D7
Pitts - burgh, Penn - syl - van - ia, but I ain't got a thing left to
G
G#dim7
D7
G
Gmaj7/F#
hock. She was peach - es, she was hon - ey and she

G6/E
G/D
D7
cost me all my mon - ey 'cause a whirl 'round the town was her
G
Am7
D7
G
Gmaj7/F#
dream. Took her danc - in', took her din - in' till her
G6/E
G/D
D7
blue eyes were shin - in' with the sights that they nev - er had
G
G7
Gdim7
G7
C
Cm
3 fr
seen. If you should run in - to a

G
D7
gol - den - haired an - gel and ask her to -
G
G7
C
night for a date, she'll tell you some -
Cm
3 fr
G
A7
where there's a rich mil - lion - aire, who is call - ing a -
D
G♯dim7
D7
G
gain a - bout eight. There's a pawn - shop on a

Gmaj7/F#
G6/E
G/D
D7
cor - ner in Pitts - burgh, Penn - syl - van - ia and I've just got to
G
Am7
D7
G
get five or ten. From the pawn - shop on a
Gmaj7/F#
G6/E
G/D
D7
cor - ner in Pitts - burgh, Penn - syl - van - ia; got - ta be with my
1
G
G#dim7
D7
2
G
G/F
Cm6/E♭
G
an - gel a - gain. There's a gain.

MENTION MY NAME IN SHEBOYGAN

Words and Music by BOB HILLIARD, DICK SANFORD and SAMMY MYSELS

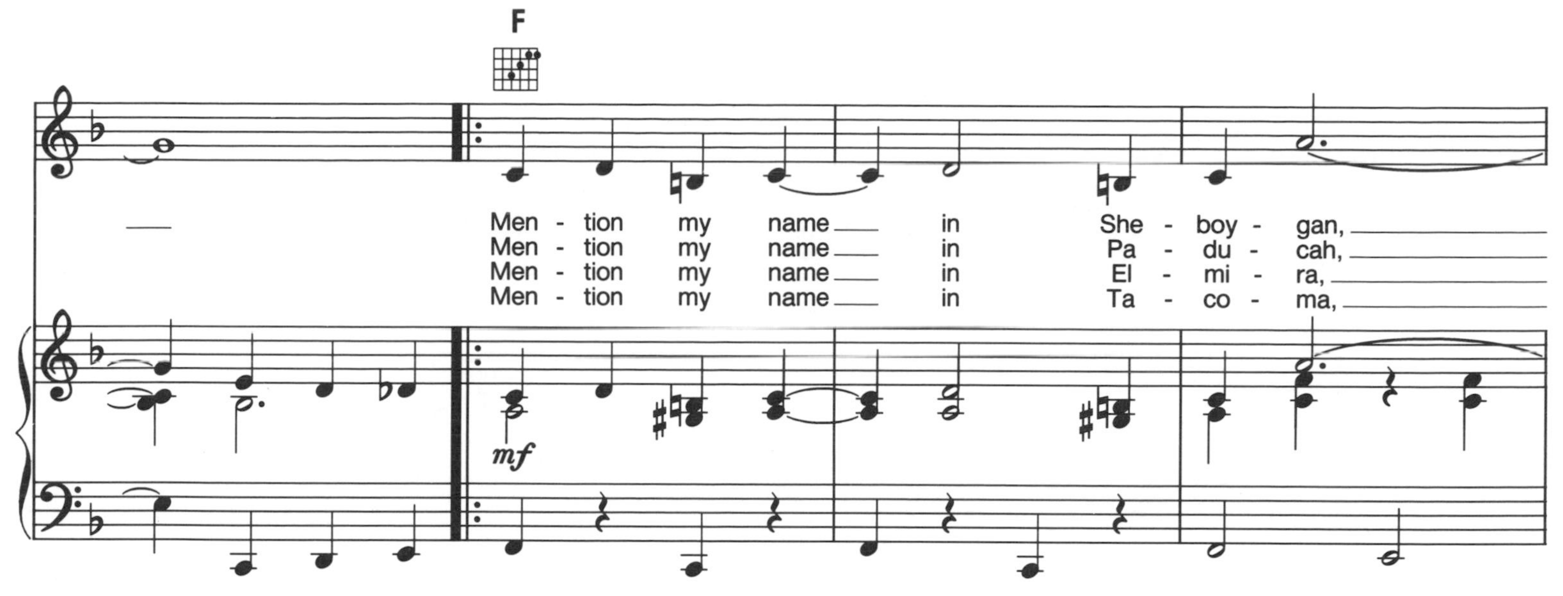
F
Men - tion my name in She - boy - gan,
Men - tion my name in Pa - du - cah,
Men - tion my name in El - mi - ra,
Men - tion my name in Ta - co - ma,
mf

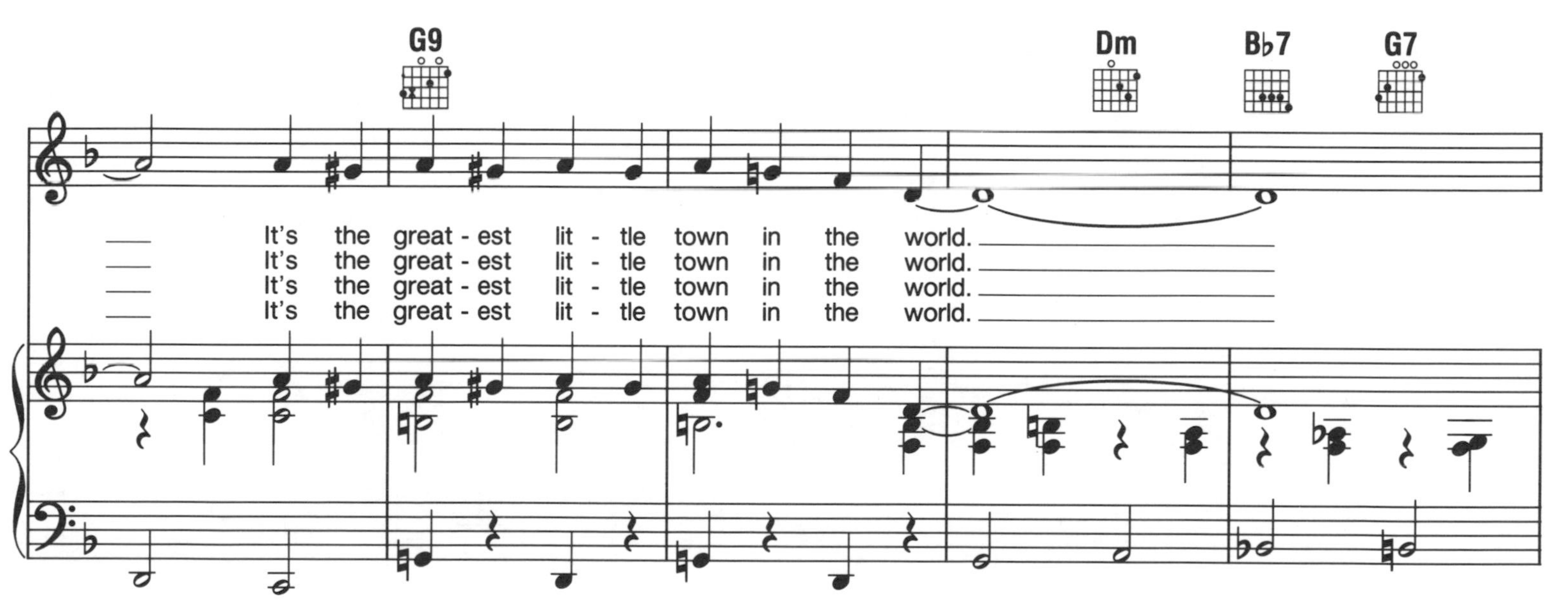
G9
Dm
B♭7
G7
It's the great - est lit - tle town in the world.
It's the great - est lit - tle town in the world.
It's the great - est lit - tle town in the world.
It's the great - est lit - tle town in the world.

C7
F
A
Dm
Just tell them all you're an old friend of mine, And
I know a gal there you'll sim - ply a - dore,
I told the May - or that he would go far, I
I know the big shots in their Cit - y Hall, They've

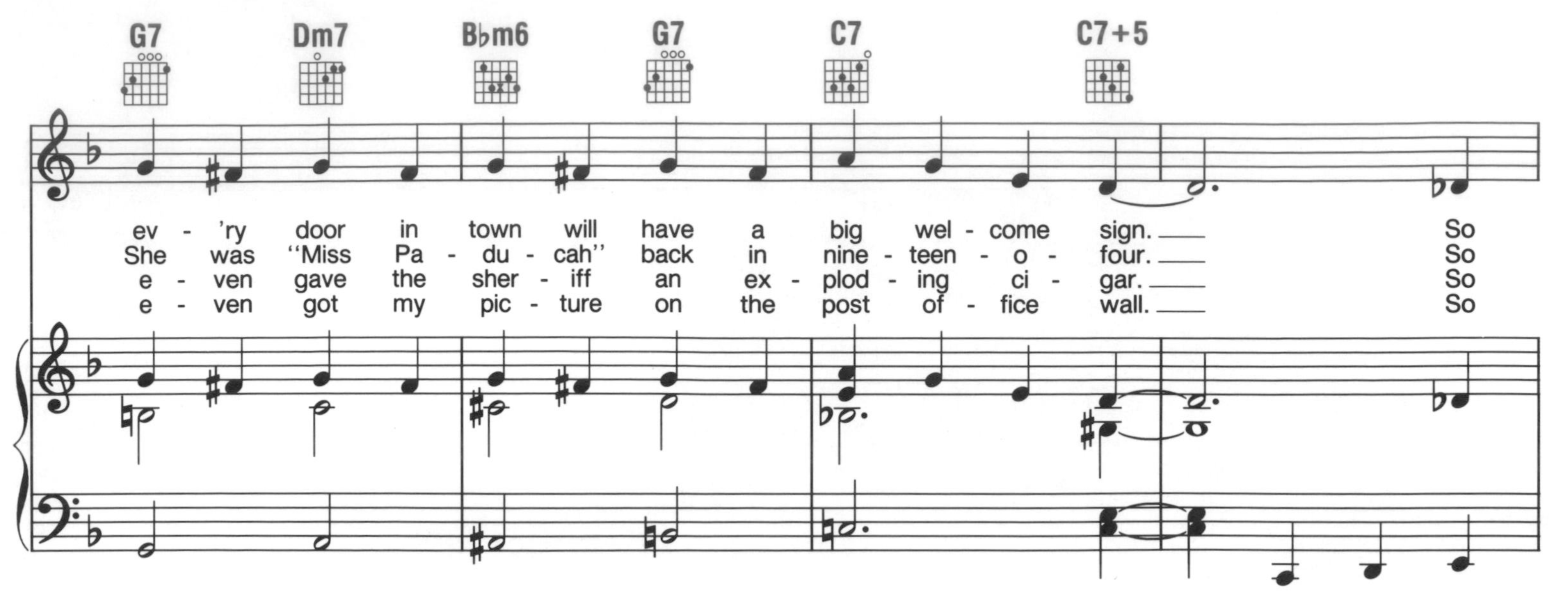
G7
Dm7
B♭m6
G7
C7
C7+5
ev - 'ry door in town will have a big wel - come sign. So
She was "Miss Pa - du - cah" back in nine - teen - o - four. So
e - ven gave the sher - iff an ex - plod - ing ci - gar. So
e - ven got my pic - ture on the post of - fice wall. So

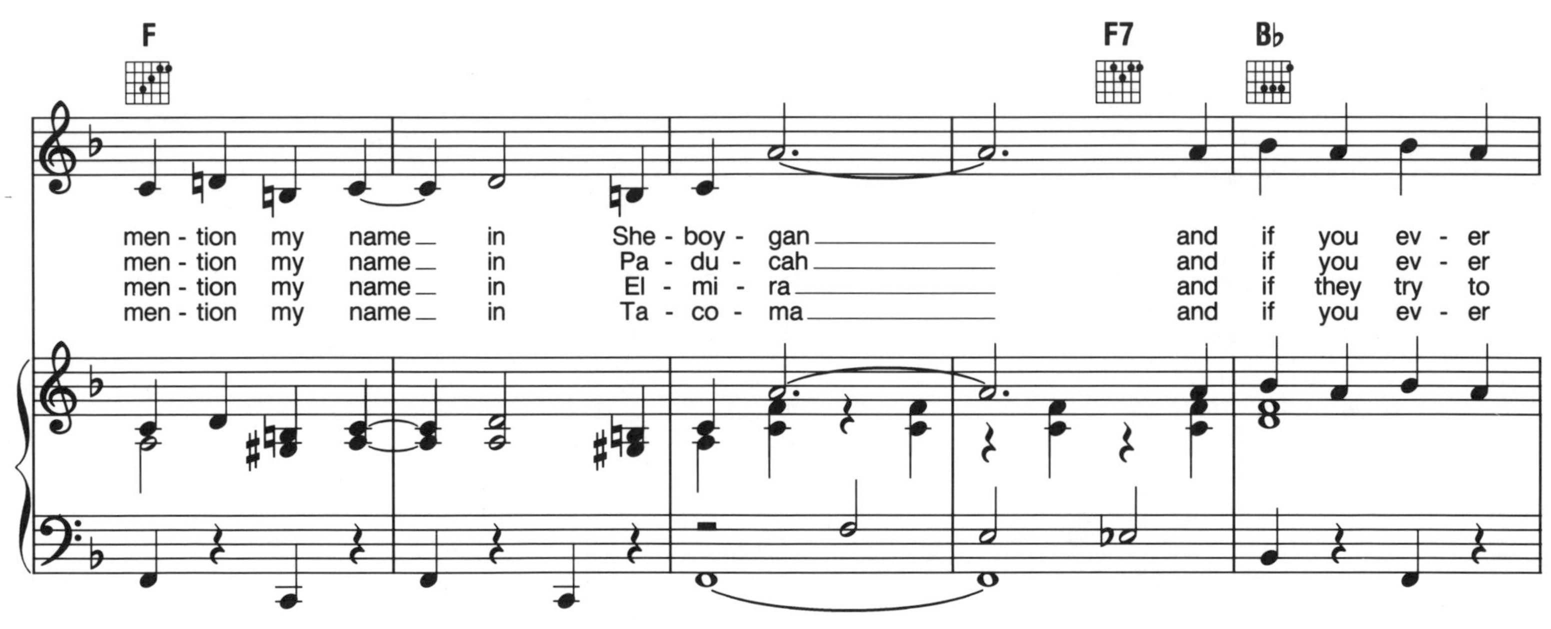
F
F7
B♭
men - tion my name in She - boy - gan and if you ev - er
men - tion my name in Pa - du - cah and if you ev - er
men - tion my name in El - mi - ra and if they try to
men - tion my name in Ta - co - ma and if you ev - er

A7
Gm7
B♭m6
get in a jam, Just men - tion my name, I said
get in a mess, Just men - tion my name, I said
put you in jail, Just men - tion my name, I said
get in a spat, Just men - tion my name, I said

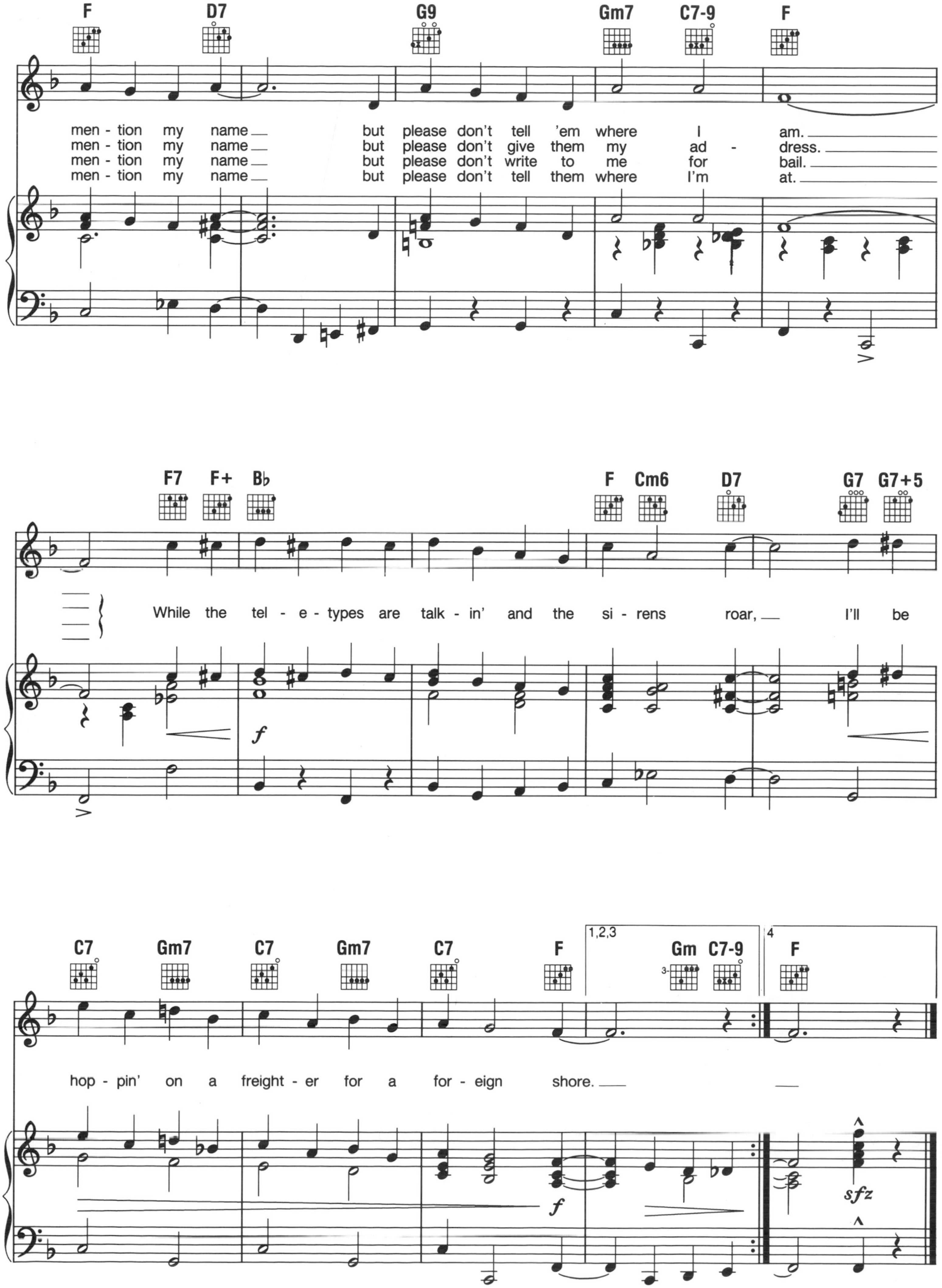

F D7 G9 Gm7 C7-9 F
men - tion my name but please don't tell 'em where I am.
men - tion my name but please don't give them my ad - dress.
men - tion my name but please don't write to me for bail.
men - tion my name but please don't tell them where I'm at.
F7 F+ B♭ F Cm6 D7 G7 G7+5
While the tel - e - types are talk - in' and the si - rens roar, I'll be
f
C7 Gm7 C7 Gm7 C7 F
1,2,3
Gm C7-9
4
F
hop - pin' on a freight - er for a for - eign shore.
f
sfz

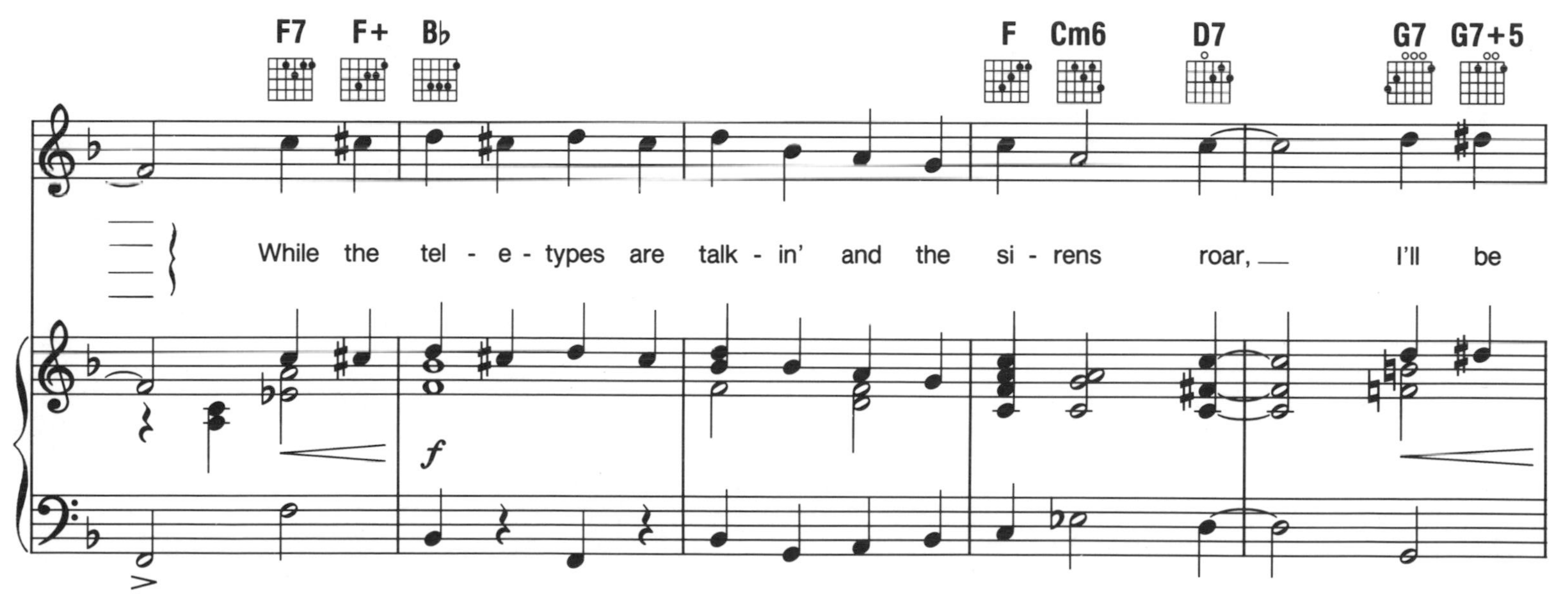

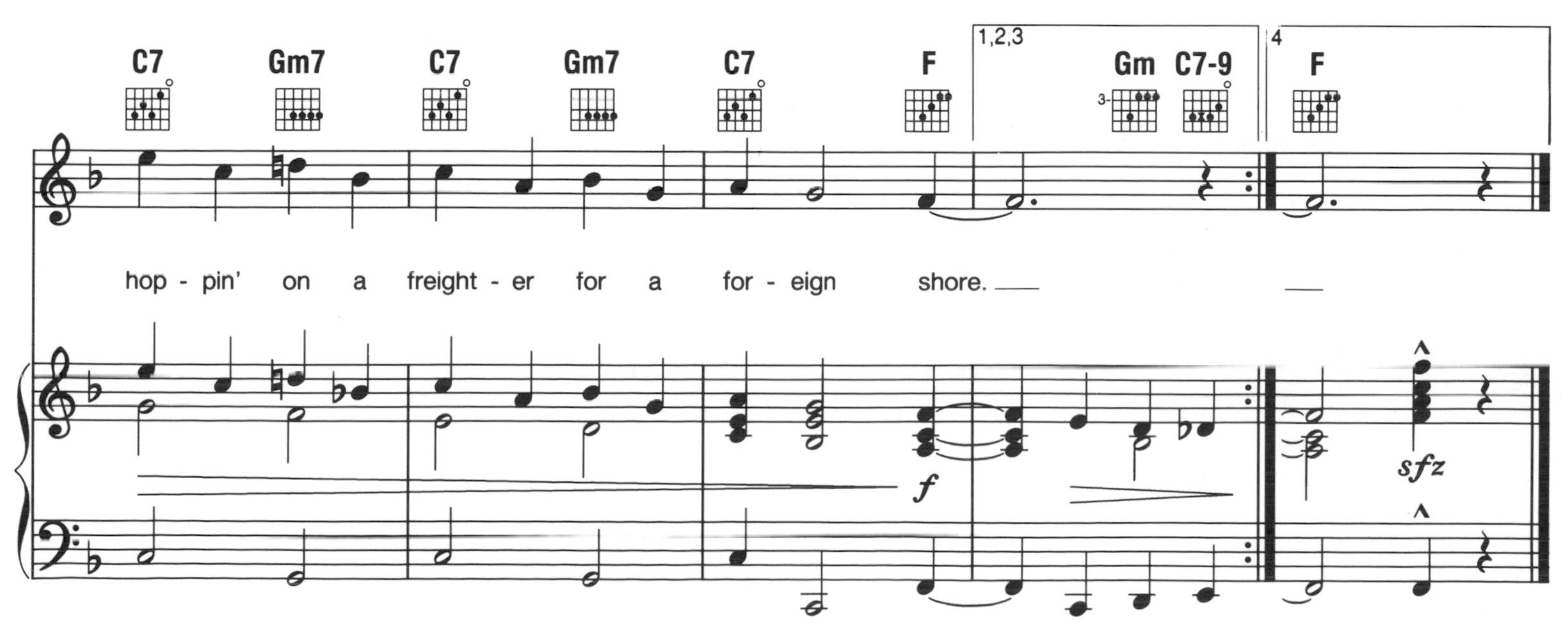

MISSISSIPPI MUD

Words and Music by JAMES CAVANAUGH
and HARRY BARRIS

Gdim7
G7
G7♯5
C
Cdim7
C
Cdim7
Un - cle Dud, it's a treat to beat your feet on the
C
Cdim7
C
Cdim7
C
Cdim
3fr
C
Cdim7
Mis - sis - sip - pi Mud. It's a treat to beat your feet on the
C
Cdim7
G7
C
A♭7
4fr
Mis - sis - sip - pi Mud." What a dance do they do,
C
C7
B7
B♭7
A7
Dm
A7
lord - y, how I'm tell - in' you. They don't need no

Dm
A7
Dm
band. They keep time by clap - pin' their hand. Just as
F
F♯dim7
C/G
A7
hap - py as a cow chew - in' on a cud when the
D7
G7
C
Fine
Am
E
Am
E7
peo - ple beat their feet on the Mis - sis - sip - pi Mud. Lord - y, how they
R.H.
Am/C
F7
Am
E7
Am
E7
Am/C
F7
play it! Good - ness, how they sway it. Un - cle

D7
G7
C
F♯dim
9fr
C
Joe, Un - cle Jim, how they pound the mire with
Eb7
D7
G7
Am
E
Am
E7
Am/C
F7
vig - or and vim. Joy! That mu - sic thrills me.
R.H.
Am
E
Am
E7
Am/C
F7
D7
Boy! It near - ly kills me. What a show when they
D.S. al Fine
G7
C
F♯dim7
C
Eb7
D7
G
G7♯5
go. Say they beat it up ei - ther fast or slow. When the

MOON OVER MIAMI

Lyric by EDGAR LESLIE
Music by JOE BURKE

Bm B♭9 D F♯7 Bm F♯7
smil - ing trou - ba - dours,. Hark to the throb - bing gui - tars.
Bm Em6 Bm Gm D E♭7 Am7 D7
Hear how the waves of - fer thun - der - ous ap - plause, Af - ter each song to the stars.
G G♯dim
Moon o - ver Mi - a - mi, You know we're wait - ing for, A lit - tle
Am7 D9 G7 C E♭9 G
love, a lit tle kiss, On Mi - a - mi shore.

MOONLIGHT IN VERMONT

Words and Music by JOHN BLACKBURN
and KARL SUESSDORF

Am7
D7+5
Gmaj7
G6
Am7
Ab9-5
Tel - e - graph ca - bles, they sing down the high - way and tra - vel each bend — in the
Gmaj7
G6
Bbm7
Eb7
Abmaj7
Ab6
road, Peo - ple who meet — in this ro - man - tic set - ting are
Bb7
Eb9
Ab
Bb7+5
Eb
Ebmaj7
Fm7
E7(#9)
so hyp - no - tized — by the love - ly ev' - ning sum - mer breeze,
Eb
Cm
Db9
Fm
Bb7
Eb
warb - ling of a mea - dow - lark, Moon - light In Ver - mont,
F9
E9
Eb
Bb7
Eb
You and I and Moon - light in Ver - mont mont.
Ped.
Ped.

OKLAHOMA

from OKLAHOMA!

Lyrics by OSCAR HAMMERSTEIN II
Music by RICHARD RODGERS

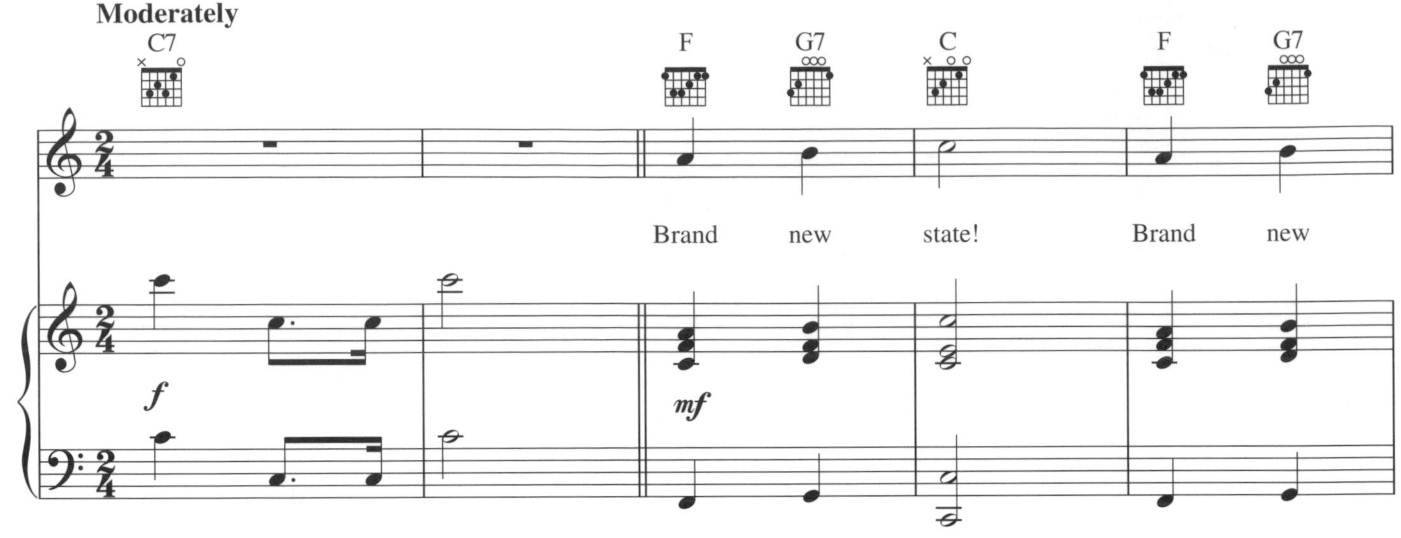

Em7(add4)
A
Em7add4)
A
Em7(add4)
A
Dm
cat - tle,
spin - ach and ter - may - ters!
Flow - ers on the
prair - ie where the June bugs zoom,
C
plen' - y of
air and plen' - y of room,
F
plen' - y of
room to swing a rope!
G7
C
Dm7
Plen' - y of
f

C/E
F
C/E
Dm7
C
Am
heart and plen' - y of hope.
G7
C
O -
F
C
G7
- k - la - hom - a where the wind comes
Gdim
G7sus
G7
C9
sweep - in' down the plain, and the wav - in'

F6
Dm7♭5
C
Csus
wheat can sure smell sweet when the wind comes
A7
D7
G7
C
right be - hind the rain.
O -
F
C
G7
- k - la - hom - a ev - 'ry night my
Gdim
G7sus
G7
C9
hon - ey lamb and I,
sit a - lone and

F6
Dm7♭5
C
talk and watch a hawk mak - in' laz - y
G7
C
F
cir - cles in the sky.
We know we be -
C
G
long to the land
and the land we be -
D7
G9
Em
G7
C
long to is grand!
And when we say
fp

F
C
D7
(Yell)
yeeow! A - yip - i - o - ee - ay!
G
D7
C
We're on - ly say - in' you're do - in'
E7
Am
Am/G
D7/F♯
D7
C
G7
fine, Ok - la - hom - a! Ok - la - hom - a
1
C
Adim7/G
G7
2
C
O. K.
K.

OLD CAPE COD

Words and Music by CLAIRE ROTHROCK,
MILT YAKUS and ALLEN JEFFREY

F7 Bb7 Eb Bbm7 Eb7 Ab Bb7 Eb Edim Fm7 Bb7-9
old Cape Cod. Wind-ing roads that seem to beck-on you, Miles of green be-neath the
Ebmaj7 Eb7 Ab Adim Eb Bbm C7 Fm7 F7
skies of blue; Church bells chim-ing on a Sun-day morn', Re-mind you of the town where
Bb7 Bb7+5 Eb Bbm7 Eb9 Ab Db9
you were born. If you spend an eve-ning, you'll want to stay, Watch-ing the moon-light on Cape Cod Bay;
Eb C7 F7 Bb7 1 Eb Cm7 Fm7 B9 Bb7 2 Eb Fm7 E7 Eb6
You're sure to fall in love with old Cape Cod. Cod.

ON BROADWAY

Words and Music by BARRY MANN, CYNTHIA WEIL,
MIKE STOLLER and JERRY LEIBER

B♭
A♭/B♭
4fr
B♭
A♭/B♭
4fr
But when you're walk - in' down that street
'cause how ya gon - na make some time
But they're dead wrong, I know they are,
B♭
A♭/B♭
4fr
B♭
C
F
E♭/F
and you ain't had e - nough to eat, the glit - ter rubs right
when all you got is one thin dime, and one thin dime won't
'cause I can play this here gui - tar, and I won't quit till
1, 2
F
E♭/F
F
E♭/F
F
E♭/F
off and you're no - where on Broad - way.
e - ven shine your shoes on Broad - way.
3
F
E♭/F
F
I'm a star on Broad - way.

PENNSYLVANIA POLKA

Words and Music by LESTER LEE
and ZEKE MANNERS

Pick out your part - ner and join in the fun
the Penn - syl - va - nia
C7♯5
8fr
F
Pol - ka.
C7
F
It start - ed in
Scran - ton, it's now num - ber one.

F7
Eb/Bb
6fr
Bb
It's bound to en - ter - tain ya.
Ev - 'ry - bod - y has a
C7
F
Abdim7
C7
ma - nia to do the pol - ka from
To Coda
F
Bbm
F
Penn - syl - va - nia.

B♭
f
While
they're
mf
danc
-
ing
ev
-
'ry
-
bod
-
y's
F7
cares
are
quick
-
ly
gone.

Sweet ro - manc - ing,
this goes on and on un - til the
B♭
dawn. They're so care -
free gay with laugh - ter,

E♭
G7/D
Cm
hap - py as can be. They stop to have a
E♭m6/G♭
F7
B♭
D♭dim7
beer, then the crowd be - gins to cheer. They
F7
C7
F7
kiss and then they start to dance a -
B♭
C7
D.C. al Coda
gain:
CODA
F
C7
F
va - nia.

A RAINY NIGHT IN GEORGIA

Chorus
Cm
3fr
Gm
3fr
Cm
3fr
A rain - y night in Geor - gia, a rain - y night in
Gm
3fr
Fm
A♭
4fr
Geor - gia; I be - lieve it's rain - in' all o - ver the
E♭
3fr
1
D♭maj7
2, 3
D♭maj7
world;
E♭maj7
3fr
D♭maj7
Fine
E♭maj7
3fr
How man - y times I've won - dered;

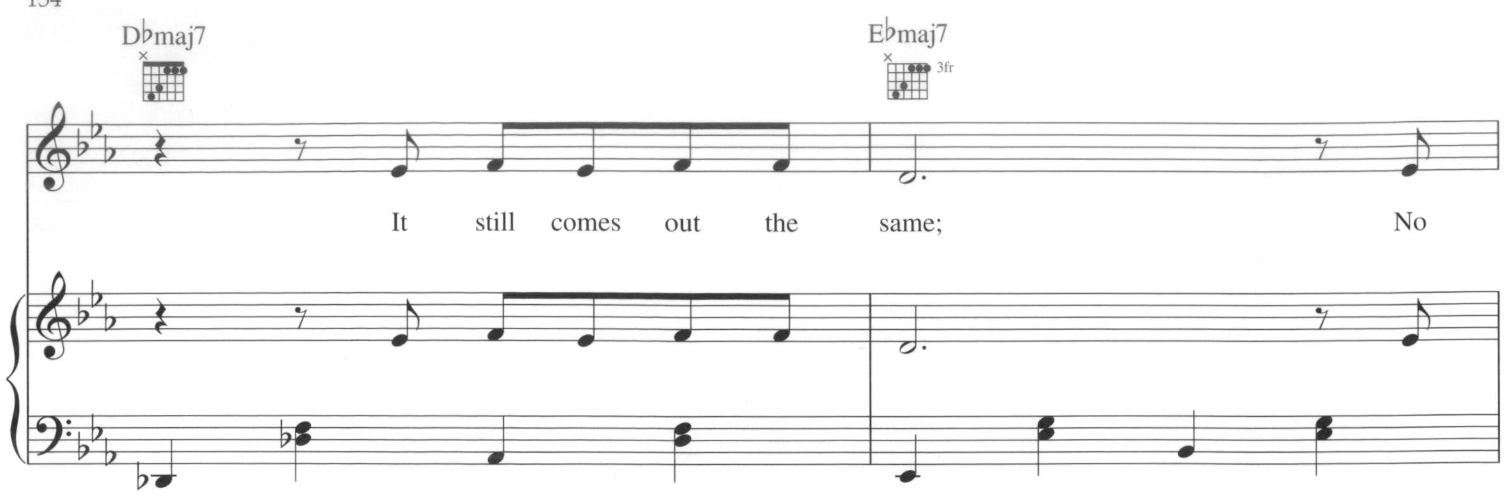

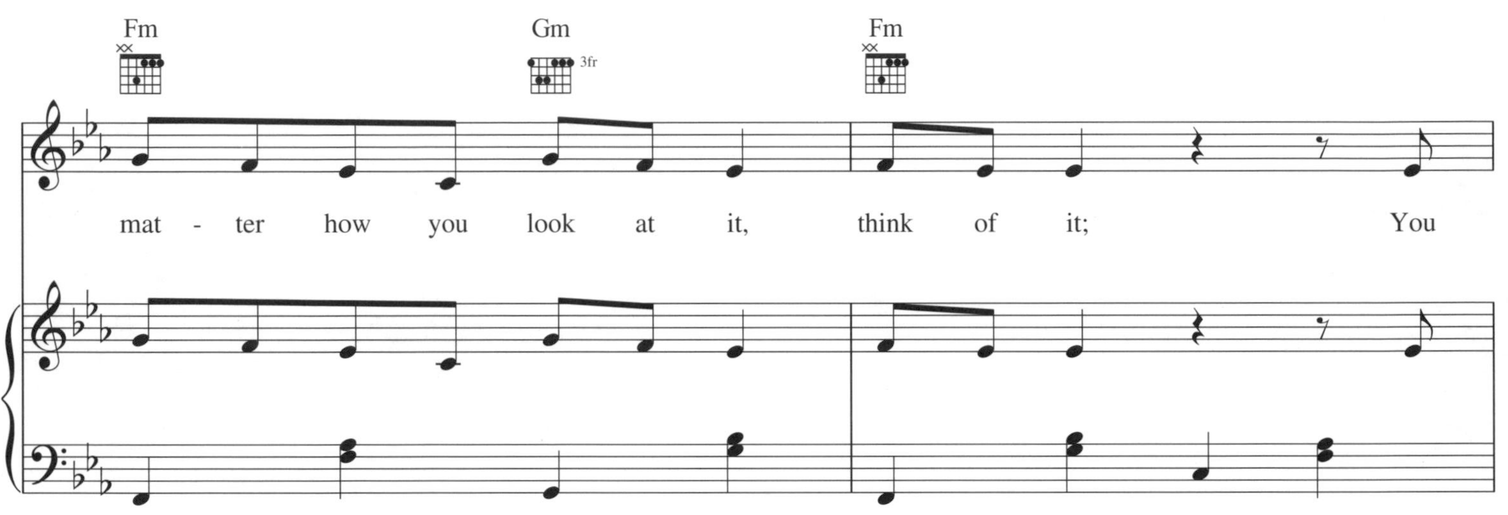

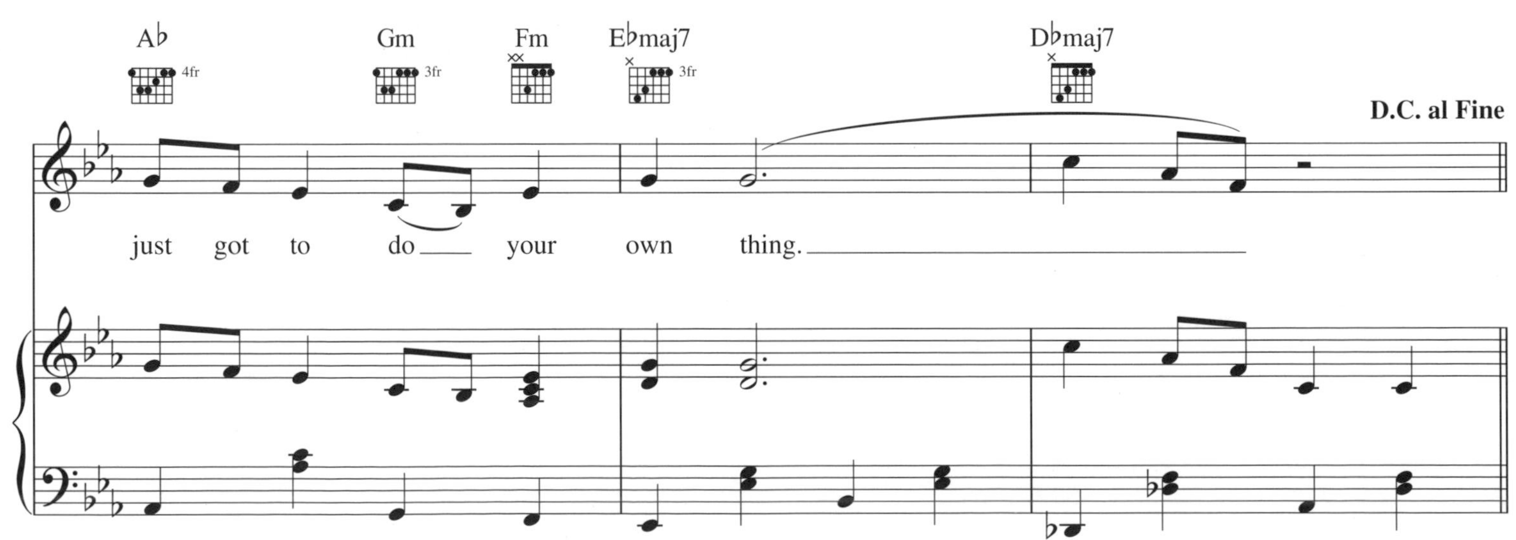

Additional Lyrics

3. I find me a place in a box car,
   So I take out my guitar to pass some time;
   Late at night when it's hard to rest,
   I hold your picture to my chest, and I'm all right;
   (To Chorus)

ROCKY MOUNTAIN HIGH

Words and Music by JOHN DENVER
and MIKE TAYLOR

E
F♯m7
yes - ter - day __ be - hind __ him ___ you might say he was born a - gain, _
say that he got cra - zy once and he tried _ to touch the sun, _
D
B
E
___ you might say he found _ a key ___ for ev - 'ry door _
___ and he lost a friend _ but kept ___ his mem - o - ry. _
F♯m7
A
B
E
When he first came to the moun -
Now he walks in qui - et sol -
life is full of won -
F♯m7
D
B
- tains ____ his life ___ was far a - way, ____ on the road _
- i - tude, the for - ests and the streams _ seek - ing
- der _____ but his heart _ still knows some fear ____ of a

E
F♯m7
and hang-in' by a song.
grace in ev-'ry step he takes.
sim-ple thing he can-not com-pre-hend.
A
B
E
But the string's al-read-y bro-ken and he
His sight has turned in-side him-self to
Why they try to tear the moun-tains down to
F♯m7
D
B
E
does-n't real-ly care, it keeps chang-in' fast and
try and un-der-stand the se-ren-i-ty of a
bring in a cou-ple more more peo-ple more
F♯m7
A
B
it don't last for long.
clear blue moun-tain lake.
scars up-on the land.
But the
And the
And the

A
B
E
Col - o - ra - do Rock - y Moun - tain high,
A
B
I've seen it rain - in' fire in the sky.
E
A
The shad-ow from the star -
Talk to God and
I know he'd be a poor -
B
E
F♯m7
Emaj7
A
- light is soft - er than a lull - a - by.
lis - ten to the cas - u - al re - ply.
- er man if he nev - er saw an ea - gle fly.

Rock - y Moun - tain high, _
E
F♯m7
A
B
To Coda
E
Rock - y Moun - tain high. _
F♯m7
1
A
B
He climbed _
2
A
B
D.S. al Coda
Now his

CODA
E
It's a
A
B
E
Col - o - ra - do Rock - y Moun - tain high,
A
B
I've seen it rain - in' fire in the sky.
E
A
Friends a - round the camp -

B
E
F♯m7
E
A
fire
and ev - 'ry - bod - y's high.
Rock - y Moun - tain high,
E
F♯m7
A
B
Repeat and Fade
Rock - y Moun - tain high,

ROUTE 66

By BOBBY TROUP

F
F13 E♭13 C13
F6
B♭9
It winds from Chi - ca - go to L. A.,
mf
F6
B♭9
more than two thou-sand miles all the way.
f
mf
F6
Gm7
C13
Get your kicks on Route Six - ty Six!
f
F
F13 E♭13 C13
F/C
B♭9
Now you go thru Saint Loo-ey Jop - lin, Mis-sour-i and
f

F/C
F7
B♭9
Ok - la - hom - a Cit - y is might - y pret - ty. You'll see Am - ar -
mf
F6/9
F
Bdim
F
Gm7
C7
il - lo, Gal - lup, New Mex - i - co; Flag - staff, Ar - i - zon - a;
3
f
Gm7
C7
F6/C
Cdim7
Gm7/C
C7
don't for - get Wi - no - na, King - man, Bar - stow, San Ber - nar - din - o. Won't
mp
cresc.
f
mf
F6
B♭9
F6
you get hip to this time - ly tip:
f

B♭9
When you make that Cal - i - for - nia trip.
mf
F6
Gm7
C13
Get your kicks on Route Six - ty Six!
f
mf
1 F
D7
C♯7
C7
no chord
If you
2 F
B♭6
Bdim7
F/C
no chord
Get your
f
Gm7
C13
F
E13 F13
kicks on Route Six - ty Six!
dim.
p
f

SAGINAW, MICHIGAN

Words and Music by DON WAYNE
and BILL ANDERSON

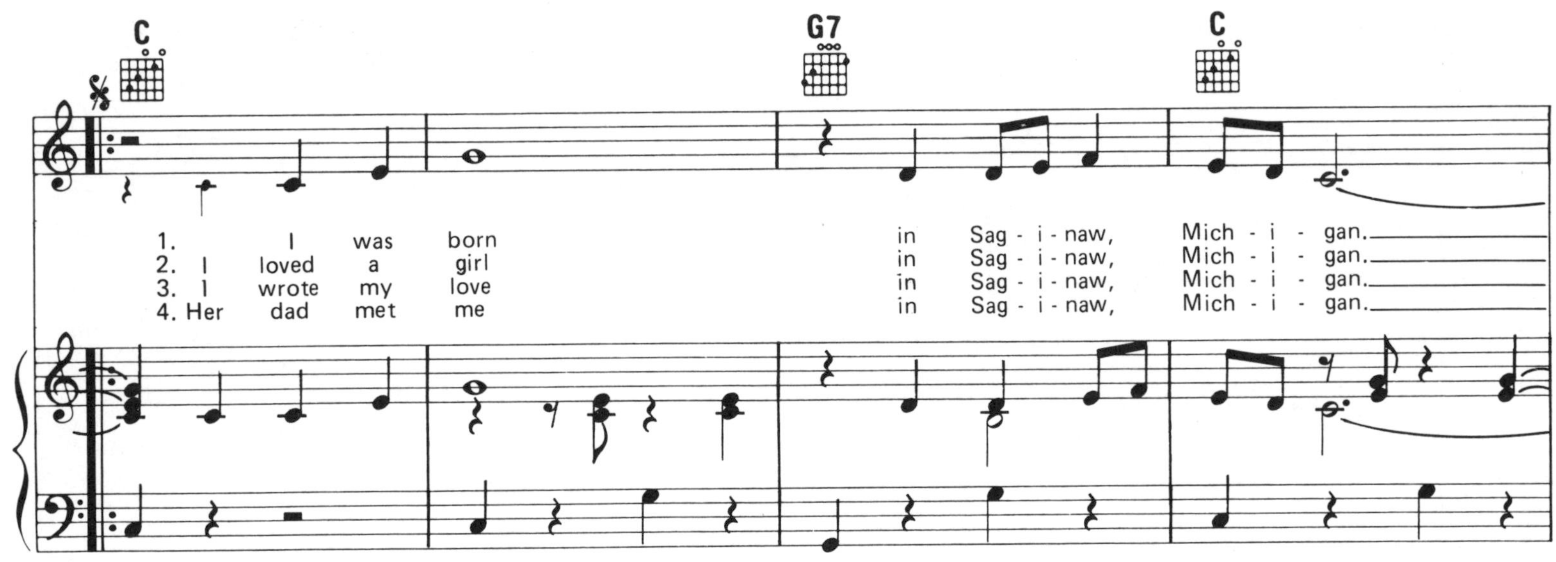

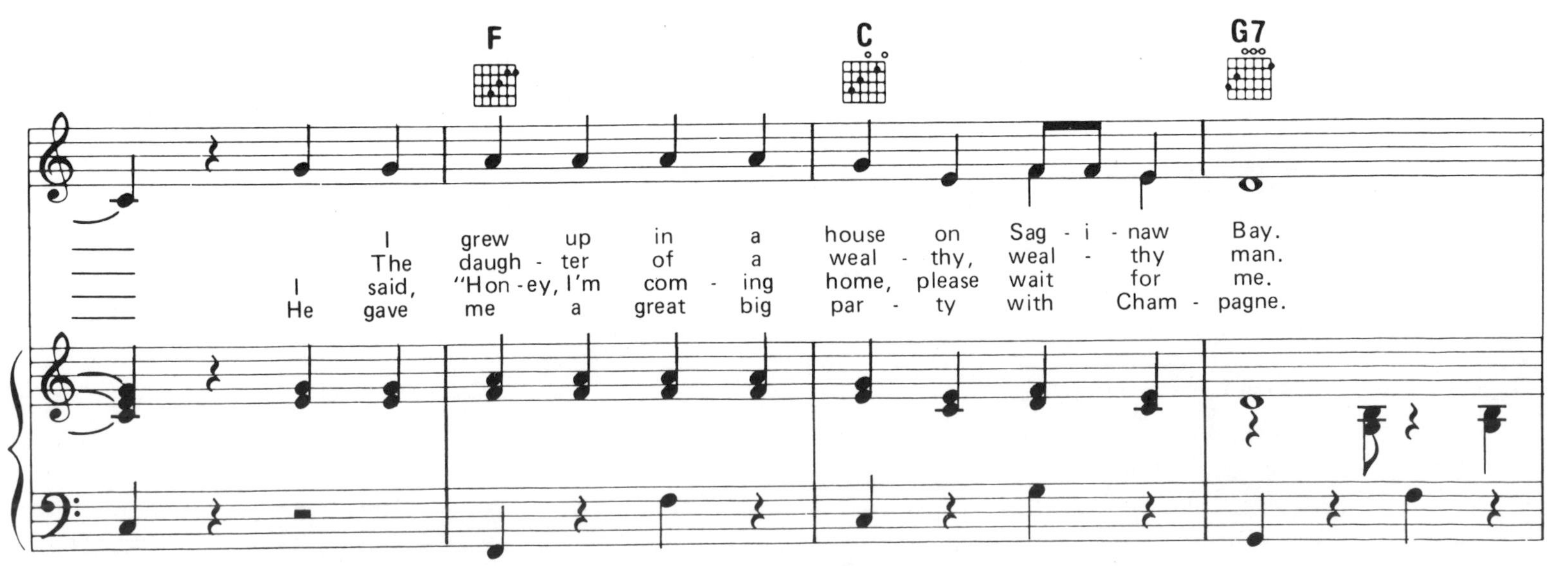

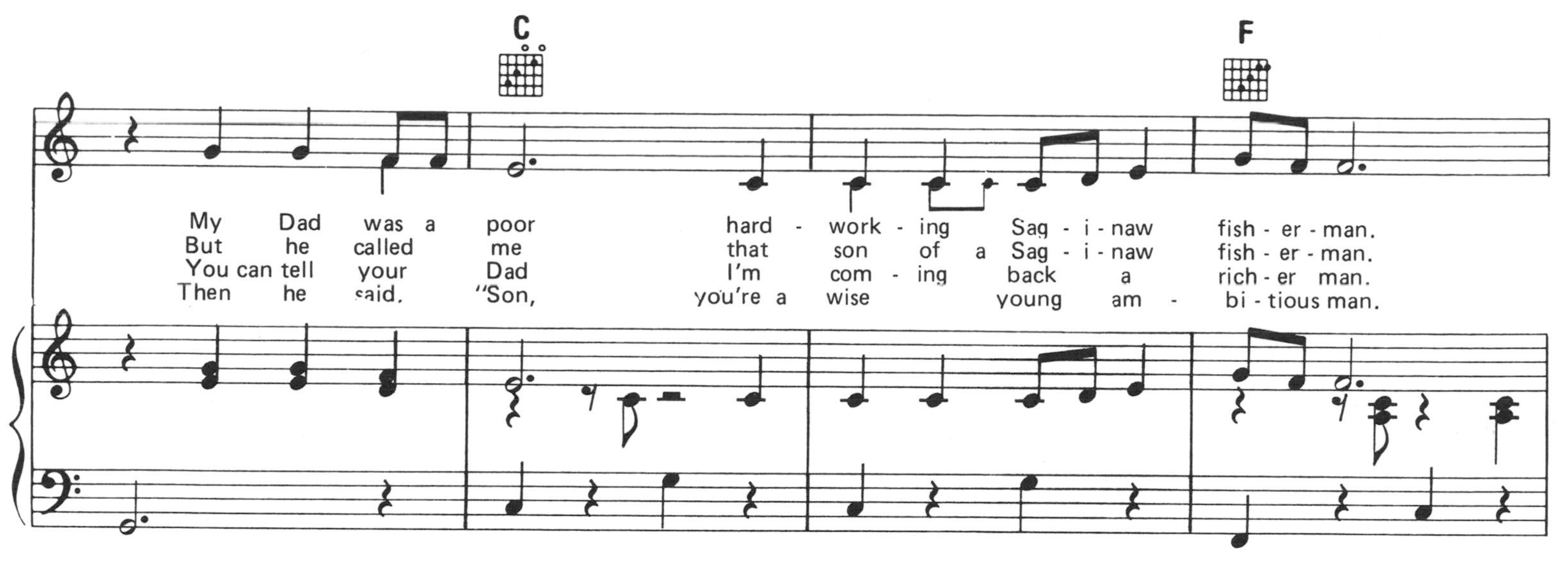
C
F
My Dad was a poor hard - work - ing Sag - i - naw fish - er - man.
But he called me that son of a Sag - i - naw fish - er - man.
You can tell your Dad I'm com - ing back a rich - er man.
Then he said, "Son, you're a wise young am - bi - tious man.

C
G7
1 C
Too man - y times he came home with too lit - tle pay.
Not good e - nough to claim his daugh - ter's
I hit the big - gest strike in Klon - dike his - to - ry.
Will you sell your Fa-ther - in - law your Klon - dike

2 C
F
hand.
claim?"
Now I'm up here in A - las - ka
Now he's up there in A - las - ka

C
G7
look - ing a - round for gold. Like a cra - zy fool I'm dig - ging in this
dig - ging in the cold, cold ground. The greed - y fool is look - ing for the
C
F
fro - zen ground so cold. But with each new day I
gold I nev - er found. It serves him right and
C
Guitar Tacet
G7
pray I'll strike it rich, and then I'll go back home and claim my
no one here is miss - ing him, Least of all the new - ly -
To Coda
C
D.S. al Coda
(With repeat)
love in Sag - i - naw, Mich - i - gan.
weds of Sag - i - naw,
CODA
C
Mich - i - gan.

ST. LOUIS BLUES

from BIRTH OF THE BLUES

Words and Music by
W.C. HANDY

G
D7
de eve - nin' sun go down.
done got ma for - tune tole.
de Dim - on Jos - eph line.
Cause my ba - by
Cause I'm most wile
He'd make a cross - eyed
D7♯5
G
he done lef dis town.
'bout ma Jel - ly Roll.
o' man go stone blind.
G7
C
G
Feel - in' to - mor - row lak Ah feel to - day
Gyp - sy done tole me, "Don't you wear no black"
Black - er than mid - night, teeth lak flags of truce
G7
C
feel to - mor - row lak Ah feel to -
yes she done tole me "Don't you wear no
black - est man in de whole St.

G
D7
D7♯5
day
I'll pack my trunk
make ma get a -
black."
Go to St. Lou - is
you can win him
Louis
black - er de ber - ry
sweet - er is the
G
Gm
3fr
Cm
3fr
C♯dim7
way.
St. Lou - is
wom - an
wid her dia - mon'
back.
Help me to
Cai - ro
make St. Louis by ma -
juice.
A - bout a
crap game
he knows a pow' - ful
D7
rings
pulls dat man roun'
self
git to Cai - ro
lot
but when work - time comes
Gm
3fr
by her a - pron
strings.
'Twant for
find ma ole friend
Jeff.
Gwine to
he's on de
dot.
Gwine to

Cm7
3fr
C♯dim7
D7
pow - der an' for store bought hair
pin ma - self close to his side
ask him for a cold ten spot
de man I love would not gone no -
if Ah flag his train I sho' can
what it takes to git it he's cer - t'n - ly
Gm
3fr
A7/E
D7
G
G6
G
G6
where. Got de St. Lou - is Blues jes as
ride. I loves dat man lak a
got. A black head - ed gal make a
G
G6
G
G6
G
C/G
G
C/G
G
C/G
G
blue as Ah can be dat
school boy loves his pie lak a
freight train jump the track said a

Extra Choruses (optional)

Lawd, a blonde-headed woman makes a good man leave the town,
I said a blonde-headed woman makes a good man leave the town,
But a red-head woman makes a boy slap his papa down.

O ashes to ashes and dust to dust,
I said ashes to ashes and dust to dust,
If my blues don't get you my jazzing must.

SAN FRANCISCO BAY BLUES

Words and Music by
JESSE FULLER

C
F
blues from my ba - by liv - in' by the San Fran - cis - co Bay.
Instrumental solo
C
C7
F
The o - cean lin - er's
C
C7
not so far a - way.
F
Did - n't mean to treat her so bad.
She was the

C
A7
best girl I ev - er have had. I
D7
said good - bye,
I can take a cry.
G
G7
I wan - na lay down and die.
I
C
F
C
ain't got a nick - el and I ain't got a lous - y dime.

C7
F
She don't come back, ain't gon - na lose my mind.
E
E7
F
Ya ev - er get back to stay,
C
A7
it's gon - na be an - oth - er brand new day,
D7
G7
C
walk - in' with ba - by down by the San Fran - cis - co Bay.

1 G
2 G
C
F
Solo ends
Sit - tin' down, look - in' from a
C
F
C
C7
back door, won-d'rin' which way to go.
F
Wom - an I'm so cra - zy 'bout, she don't love me no more.
C
F
Think I'll catch me the freight train

C
A7
'cause I'm feel - in' blue,
D7
ride all way to the end of the line,
G
G7
C
F
think - in' on - ly of you.
Mean - while, liv - in' in the
C
F
C
C7
cit - y,
just a - bout go in - sane.

F
E7
All I heard my ba - by, Lord, wish - in' you would call my name.
F
If I ev - er get back to stay, it's gon - na
C
A7
be an - oth - er brand new day,
D7
G7
walk - in' with my ba - by down by the San Fran - cis - co Bay,

C
A7
D7
hey, hey,
walk - in' with my ba - by down
G7
C
A7
by the San Fran - cis - co Bay,
Yeah, I'm
D7
G7
C
F
walk - in' with my ba - by down by the San Fran-cis - co Bay.
C
G
C
C7

SEATTLE

from the Television Series HERE COME THE BRIDES

Words and Music by ERNIE SHELDON, JACK KELLER
and HUGO MONTENEGRO

Em D G D Em D Em D
hopes and full of fears, full of laugh - ter full of tears, full of dreams
G D C/E C D G D/F♯ Em7 C D
to last the years in Se - at - tle, in Se -
G D/F♯ To Coda G G Em
at - tle.
When it's time to leave your home and your
When you find your own true love you will
Ifl you ev - er fall in love with a
C Am7 Am7/D D G Em
loved ones, it's the hard - est thing a girl boy can ev - er do.
know it, by his her smile, by the look in his her eye.
log - ger, there is some - thing you will have to un - der - stand.

F
D7
Am7/D
D
G
Em
And you pray that you will find some - one
Scent of pine trees in the air nev - er
For as much as he may care, you will
C
D7
C
D
C/E
D7/F#
C/D
D
strong and good
warm and sweet
and kind,
knew a day so fair.
al - ways have to share,
but you're not sure what's wait - ing there for
It makes you feel so good that you could
his love with his green moun - tain
1,2
3
D.S. al Coda
G
G/D
you.
cry.
The blu - est sky
land.
The blu - est sky
CODA
G
D/F#
Em7
G/D
G
C
G
In Se - at - tle,
in Se - at - tle.

TENNESSEE WALTZ

Words and Music by REDD STEWART
and PEE WEE KING

G
G7
duced him to my loved one and ___ while they were ___
C
G
D7
waltz - ing my friend stole my sweet - heart from
G
B7
me. ___ I re - mem - ber the night and the
C
G
Ten - nes - see Waltz. Now I know just how

D7
G
much I have lost.
Yes I lost my lit - tle
G7
C
dar - lin' the night they were play - ing the
G
D7
1
G
beau - ti - ful Ten - nes - see Waltz.
2
G
I was Waltz.

SIOUX CITY SUE

Words by RAY FREEDMAN
Music by DICK THOMAS

Chorus
F
G7
SIOUX CIT - Y SUE,
SIOUX CIT - Y SUE,
C7
Your hair is red, your eyes are blue, I'd
F
Bb
F
C7
F
swap my horse and dog for you.
SIOUX CIT - Y SUE,
G7
C7
Cdim
C7
Ddim
C7
SIOUX CIT - Y SUE,
There ain't no gal as true As my
1-2 Repeat from Verse
Optional to repeat Chorus
3 Fine
F
F
Ddim
C7
F
sweet SIOUX CIT - Y SUE.
I
Now
SUE.
SUE.

VIVA LAS VEGAS

Words and Music by DOC POMUS
and MORT SHUMAN

Em
wait - in' out there___ And they're all liv - in' de - vil may care___ And
rou - lette wheel___ A for - tune won and lost on ev - 'ry deal___
I'm just the de - vil with love to spare___
All you need's a strong heart and a nerve of steel___
C
Vi - va___ Las
Vi - va___ Las
G
Ve - gas,
Ve - gas,
C
Vi - va___ Las Ve - gas
Vi - va,___ Las
1 G
2 G
Ve - gas.
C
Vi - va Las Ve - gas with your ne - on flash - in' and your one arm ban - dits crash - in'
G
All those hopes down the drain___
C
Vi - va Las Ve - gas turn - in' day in - to

A7
night time, turn - in' night in - to day time, If you see it once you'll ne - ver be the
D7
G D7 G
same a - gain. I'm gon - na keep on the
G
run, I'm gon - na have me some fun if it costs me my ve - ry last dime
If I wind up broke well I'll al - ways re - mem - ber that I had a
B7 Em
swing - in' time. I'm gon - na give it ev - 'ry - thing I've got

La - dy luck please let the dice stay hot
Let me shoot a se - ven with ev - 'ry shot.
C
G
Vi - va Las Ve - gas,
C
G
Vi - va Las Ve - gas,
C
Vi - va Las
G
Ve - gas,
C
Vi - va,
D7
Vi - va Las
G
Ve - gas.
G6

'WAY DOWN YONDER IN NEW ORLEANS

Words and Music by HENRY CREAMER
and J. TURNER LAYTON

B♭ F/A G7 C7
ain't go - in' West, I ain't go - in' o - ver the cuck - oo's nest. I'm
ain't think - in' that, I can - not be think - in' a - bout your hat. My
F B♭ D7/A A♭7♭5 G7
bound for the town that I love best, where life is one sweet
heart does not start to pit - a - pat, un - less I hear this
C7 C7 Gm9 C7
song:
song:
'Way down yon - der in New Or - leans,
mf
Fmaj7 C7 F♯dim7
in the land of dream - y scenes, there's a gar - den of E - den

C7
C7♯5
F
F♯dim
C7
that's what I mean
Cre - ole ba - bies with
Gm9
3fr
C7
Fmaj7
flash - ing eyes
soft - ly whis - per with ten - der sighs,
F7
B♭
F7♯5
"Stop! Oh! won't you give your la - dy fair a lit - tle
B♭
A7
A♭7
4fr
G7
smile?" Stop! You bet your life you'll lin - ger there

C7
Cdim7
C7
F
a lit - tle while.
There is Heav - en right
They've got an - gels right
Dm
F
D♭7
here on earth
with those beau - ti - ful queens
here on earth
wear - ing lit - tle blue jeans
F
F♯dim7
C7
1
F
F♯dim7
'way down yon - der in New Or - leans.
Gm7
C7♭9
Cdim7
2
F
Dm9
Gm9
G♭7
F6
leans.

YOU CAME A LONG WAY FROM ST. LOUIS

2
Fm7 Emaj7 Ebmaj7
Tacet
Abmaj7 Bbm7 Fm7-5
You blew in from the mid-dle west and cer-tain-ly im-pressed the pop-u-la-tion
Eb6
here a-bouts.
Tacet
Abmaj7 Bbm7 Fm7-5
Well, ba-by, I got news for you, I'm from Mis-sou-ri, too, so natch-er-ly I
Bb11 Bb7
got my doubts.
Tacet
You got 'em drop-pin' by the way-side,
Eb6 Fm7 Emaj7 Ebmaj7
Tacet
a feel-in' I ain't gon-na
Eb6 Dbmaj7 Dmaj7 Ebmaj7
know.
Tacet
You Came A Long Way From St. Lou-is, but ba-by, you still
Ebmaj7 Fm7 Gm7
Abmaj7 Bb13 Eb6
got a long way to go.
Eb7

Get more BANG for your buck! with budgetbooks

These value-priced collections feature 352 pages of piano/vocal/guitar arrangements. With at least 70 hit songs in each book for only $12.95, you pay 18 cents or less for each song!

BROADWAY SONGS

This jam-packed collection features 73 songs from 56 shows, including *Annie Get Your Gun, Beauty and the Beast, Cabaret, The Full Monty, Jekyll & Hyde, Les Misérables, The Music Man, Oklahoma!*, and more. Songs include: Any Dream Will Do • Cabaret • Consider Yourself • Footloose • Getting to Know You • I Dreamed a Dream • The Impossible Dream (The Quest) • Love Changes Everything • One • People • Summer Nights • The Surrey with the Fringe on Top • With One Look • You'll Never Walk Alone • and more.

00310832 P/V/G $12.95

CHRISTMAS SONGS

Save some money this Christmas with this fabulous budget-priced collection of 100 holiday favorites! Includes: All I Want for Christmas Is You • Away in a Manger • Baby, It's Cold Outside • Caroling, Caroling • The Christmas Song (Chestnuts Roasting on an Open Fire) • Christmas Time Is Here • Feliz Navidad • The First Noel • Frosty the Snow Man • Grandma Got Run Over by a Reindeer • Happy Holiday • I'll Be Home for Christmas • I've Got My Love to Keep Me Warm • It's Beginning to Look Like Christmas • Jesus Born on This Day • Last Christmas • Let It Snow! Let It Snow! Let It Snow! • Merry Christmas, Darling • Merry Christmas, Baby • Miss You Most at Christmas Time • O Holy Night • Please Come Home for Christmas • Rockin' Around the Christmas Tree • Rudolph the Red-Nosed Reindeer • Silver Bells • Some Children See Him • We Need a Little Christmas • What Child Is This? • Wonderful Christmastime • and more.

00310887 P/V/G $12.95

CLASSIC ROCK

A priceless collection of 70 of rock's best at a price that can't be beat! Includes: Ballroom Blitz • Bohemian Rhapsody • Come Sail Away • Don't Do Me Like That • Don't Fear the Reaper • Don't Stand So Close to Me • Eye in the Sky • Gloria • Heroes • Maggie May • New Kid in Town • Owner of a Lonely Heart • Pink Houses • Rhiannon • Roxanne • Summer of '69 • Sweet Emotion • Walk of Life • Walk on the Wild Side • Wild Thing • You Really Got Me • and more.

00310906 P/V/G $12.95

COUNTRY SONGS

A great collection of 90 songs, including: Abilene • All My Ex's Live in Texas • Always on My Mind • Amazed • Blue Eyes Crying in the Rain • Boot Scootin' Boogie • Breathe • By the Time I Get to Phoenix • The Chair • Cowboy Take Me Away • Down at the Twist and Shout • Elvira • Friends in Low Places • The Greatest Man I Never Knew • Help Me Make It Through the Night • Hey, Good Lookin' • Lucille • Mammas Don't Let Your Babies Grow Up to Be Cowboys • Okie from Muskogee • Sixteen Tons • Walkin' After Midnight • You Are My Sunshine • and many more!

00310833 P/V/G $12.95

JAZZ STANDARDS

A collection of over 80 jazz classics. Includes: Alfie • Alright, Okay, You Win • Always in My Heart (Siempre En Mi Corazón) • Autumn in New York • Bewitched • Blue Skies • Body and Soul • Cherokee (Indian Love Song) • Do Nothin' Till You Hear from Me • Fever • Fly Me to the Moon (In Other Words) • Good Morning Heartache • Harlem Nocturne • I'll Be Seeing You • In the Mood • Isn't It Romantic? • Lazy Afternoon • Lover • Manhattan • Mona Lisa • Stella by Starlight • When Sunny Gets Blue • and more.

00310830 P/V/G $12.95

LOVE SONGS

This collection of over 70 favorite love songs includes: And I Love Her • Crazy • Endless Love • Fields of Gold • I Just Called to Say I Love You • I'll Be There • Longer • (You Make Me Feel Like) A Natural Woman • Still • Wonderful Tonight • You Are So Beautiful • You Are the Sunshine of My Life • and more.

00310834 P/V/G $12.95

MOVIE SONGS

Over 70 memorable movie moments, including: Almost Paradise • Also Sprach Zarathustra, Opening Theme • Cole's Song • The Crying Game • Funny Girl • I Say a Little Prayer • Il Postino (The Postman) • Jailhouse Rock • Psycho (Prelude) • Puttin' On the Ritz • She • Southampton • Take My Breath Away (Love Theme) • Theme from "Terms of Endearment" • Up Where We Belong • The Way We Were • Where the Boys Are • and more.

00310831 P/V/G $12.95

POP/ROCK

This great collection of 75 top pop hits features: Adia • Angel • Back in the High Life Again • Barbara Ann • Crimson and Clover • Don't Cry Out Loud • Dust in the Wind • Hero • I Hope You Dance • If You're Gone • Jack and Diane • Lady Marmalade • Mony, Mony • Respect • Stand by Me • Tequila • Vision of Love • We Got the Beat • What's Going On • You Sang to Me • and more!

00310835 P/V/G $12.95

Prices, contents & availability subject to change without notice.

FOR MORE INFORMATION, SEE YOUR LOCAL MUSIC DEALER, OR WRITE TO:

7777 W. BLUEMOUND RD. P.O. BOX 13819 MILWAUKEE, WI 53213

Visit Hal Leonard Online at
www.halleonard.com